POLICY AND PRACTICE IN EDUCATION

NUMBER TWELVE

St John

GENDER INEQUALITY Services
RAISING PUPIL ACHIEVEMENT

POLICY AND PRACTICE IN EDUCATION

POLICY AND PRACTICE IN EDUCATION
SERIES EDITORS
JIM O'BRIEN and CHRISTINE FORDE

TACKLING GENDER INEQUALITY, RAISING PUPIL ACHIEVEMENT

Edited by
Christine Forde

Professor of Education
University of Glasgow

DUNEDIN ACADEMIC PRESS
EDINBURGH

Published by
Dunedin Academic Press Ltd
Hudson House
8 Albany Street
Edinburgh EH1 3QB
Scotland

ISBN 978-1-903765-75-3
ISSN 1479-6910

British Library Cataloguing in Publication Data
A catalogue record for this book is available from the British Library

Typeset by Makar Publishing Production
Printed in Great Britain by Cpod, Trowbridge, Wiltshire

CONTENTS

SERIES EDITORS' INTRODUCTION

This new volume in our Policy and Practice series deals with questions raised by the specific issue of gender in education, which is both complex and complicated. Should education and schooling differentiate on gender grounds? If so, how might this be achieved in practice, particularly through classroom strategies, and with what expected outcomes? The discussion is located in a consideration of the international literature on gender-related issues. It reflects local work and understandings derived from a recent research project undertaken on behalf of the Scottish Executive which demonstrates the political as well as the educational importance of the theme. Christine Forde and her contributors, based at the Universities of Glasgow and Strathclyde, succeed in raising the pertinent issues by considering how the question of gender relates to other important factors such as social class, race, sexuality and disability. The contributors describe and critique a range of strategies that may be adopted by schools and early years' establishments to raise the achievement of both girls and boys within the overall framework of inclusive education. The book draws on a number of case studies conducted as part of their research and the contributors appraise some of the approaches and strategies being adopted now.

Dr Jim O'Brien
Vice Dean and Director,
Centre for Educational Leadership,
Moray House School of Education,
The University of Edinburgh

Professor Christine Forde
Department of Educational Studies,
Faculty of Education,
The University of Glasgow

ACKNOWLEDGEMENTS

The authors gratefully acknowledge the support of the Scottish Executive Education Department in funding the research project Strategies to Address Gender Inequalities in Scottish Schools. The authors wish to thank the local authorities, schools and pre-5 establishments and the staff, pupils and parents who generously gave up their time and participated in the research. Our thanks are also due to our former colleague, Maria Cassidy, who undertook one of the early years' case studies in this research project.

CONTRIBUTORS

Professor Rae Condie, Deputy Principal, University of Strathclyde.

Dr Alastair McPhee, Reader in Education, Faculty of Education, University of Glasgow.

Dr Jean Kane, Senior Lecturer, Faculty of Education, University of Glasgow.

Dr George Head, Senior Lecturer, Faculty of Education, University of Glasgow.

Professor Christine Forde, Faculty of Education, University of Glasgow.

CHAPTER 1

GENDER IN AN INCLUSION AGENDA: BOYS FIRST, GIRLS FIRST?

Christine Forde

Introduction

Inclusion is a key theme in social and educational policy in Scotland. The more general use of the term 'inclusion' points to a political position that advocates for concerted efforts to combat social and economic disadvantage and to challenge discrimination and exclusion in every sphere of life. In education the concept of 'inclusion' has much to commend it as it is centrally concerned with social justice, fairness and equality. This concept has the benefit of enabling us to appreciate the varied range of social factors such as gender, poverty, disability, sexuality, race and ethnicity that have the cumulative effect of limiting aspiration and opportunities within education. However, we have to balance the need to challenge discrimination and exclusion on a broad front with an appreciation of particular issues related to specific social factors. In this book we consider the questions raised by the specific issue of gender in education and discuss some of the strategies schools and early years' establishments can adopt to raise the achievement of both girls and boys within the overall framework of inclusive education. To do so we draw on a recently completed Scottish Executive Education Department (SEED) funded research project (Condie et al., 2005) investigating strategies to address gender inequality in Scottish schools. In this book we draw from a number of case studies and examine critically some of the strategies being adopted currently in schools. We also consider the question of the direction of policy in the complex area of gender and education. In this first chapter we examine some of the issues related to gender inequality by firstly, considering some of the trends in education and then by exploring different approaches to the issue of gender in education.

Is gender still important?

With the development of second wave feminism in the 1970s and the efforts of activists in the UK, the issue of gender became a concern for both educational practitioners and policy makers because of the differential experiences and outcomes for boys and girls in education. At that point there existed gender-differentiated curricula, there were concerns about the underachievement and low aspirations of groups of girls and their marginalised position in classrooms. Studies by feminist educationalists such as Stanworth (1983) and Spender (1982) were highly influential in highlighting the disadvantages girls and women experienced in education from early childhood education to higher education. In line with feminist aspirations for the liberation of women, the early focus was clearly on addressing the needs of girls whose expectations and achievements had historically been limited by deterministic notions of girls' abilities and interests. Feminist projects such as *Girls into Science and Technology* (Whyte, 1986) very much focused on challenging the barriers experienced by women and girls in their educational careers. From these early efforts policy and practice has continued to evolve.

Kenway (2004) depicts the evolution historically of debates and strategies and highlights the tensions between the need for concrete approaches within an educational setting and the philosophic and political debates about identity stemming from post-structuralist and post-modernist perspectives. Despite the success of early reforms in the educational system in Australia – reforms mirrored in other education systems – more recent preoccupations, particularly about identity, have had far less impact. These debates about identity seem to be distant from and perhaps lack relevance to the practical demands of everyday life in the classrooms. This gap between the concerns of practitioners and the focus of research and theoretical discussions on gender and education has allowed the development of what Kenway describes as 'gender fundamentalism' in which policy has moved from a concern that girls can access the same educational opportunities as their male peers to the predominant focus in popular discourses on the seeming disengagement of boys from education and their falling attainment relative to that of girls.

Undoubtedly there have been significant advances made by girls and women in education – both as learners and educational professionals – which might suggest that we no longer need be concerned with gender; there is the view that 'gender has been done'. Further, the more recent improvement in the attainment of girls relative to that of boys (Tinklin *et al.*, 2001; Tinklin, 2003) has led to the idea of 'too much, too far' – the view that the strategies to enhance the achievement of girls have led to the underperformance of boys. Sommers's (2000) work is an extreme example of this position in which she claims that as a result of feminist efforts to improve the achievement of girls in education, boys are now 'politically incorrect'. Sommers demands a return to forms of education such as drilling, rote learning and strict discipline which, in her view, boys need.

To claim that gender has been 'done' or that gender reforms have 'gone too far' is misguided on a number of counts. Firstly, this position does not recognise that there are significant groups of girls and women who continue to experience educational disadvantage and exclusion and the current emphasis on boys' attainment does nothing to address these areas. Secondly and more fundamentally, it would seem that when the needs and issues concerning one gender are being addressed, this is seen as inevitably disadvantaging the other. Such an approach simply pits one gender against the other and does nothing to ask which boys or which girls are being disadvantaged or how the particular barriers to learning that these groups of girls and boys experience might be removed. Given what seems to be an almost inevitable tension between the learning needs of girls and of boys we must, firstly, look closely at the gender trends and secondly, consider alternative ways of approaching gender in education.

Patterns of gender inequalities in attainment

Although the origins of gender debates in education focused on the underachievement of girls, since the mid-1990s data – principally from public assessment systems – has caused the focus to shift to boys. The apparent underachievement of boys in national examinations is a trend noted in all UK education systems, as well as in those of the USA, Canada, Australia and New Zealand (Francis, 1999; Jackson, 2002). These gender trends in performance are evident from early years. Murphy and Elwood (1999) note that the construction of gender identity starts at a very early age, early enough for differences to be apparent in baseline assessments in Primary One in English schools. Davies and Brember (1995) report that, even at that early stage, there are signs of boys being more vulnerable to becoming disaffected. They also note that, by the end of primary school, girls were less positive about mathematics than when they started school and boys were less positive than girls about reading and writing. The decline in boys' attitudes to school was related to discipline. They were less careful about rules than girls and more indifferent to being reprimanded. Although girls seem to fare better, there is evidence, though, as Murphy and Elwood (1999) argue, that this conformity creates lower expectations of girls' ability, whereas the more challenging, ebullient and risk-taking behaviour of boys is viewed by teachers as indicative of higher levels of ability.

The issue of gender remains significant in education today for a variety of reasons: the gendered patterns in subject choice, classroom interaction, educational attainment particularly in national examinations, exclusion and referral rates (Scottish Executive Education Department (SEED), 2004; Head *et al.*, 2002) – all continue to reveal different experiences and outcomes for girls and boys in education. Further, the issue of gender has come to the forefront in the teaching profession as increasingly across all sectors from pre-5 to secondary education women make up nearly 70% of the workforce (Tett and Riddell, 2006). In Scotland, a number of recent studies (Croxford, 1999; Wilkinson *et al.*, 1999; Tinklin *et al.*, 2001) have included second- ary analyses of a range of quantitative data from the Scottish Qualifications Authority, Assessment of Achievement Programme, Scottish Executive's Statistical Bulletins and Baseline Assessment Programmes. These analyses have demonstrated that whilst levels of attainment have increased overall since the 1970s, average levels of attainment for boys are less than for girls at all stages and across almost all areas of the curriculum. Commentators are careful to point out that, though the picture in some curricular areas such as literacy is clear, in areas such as mathematics the relative average perform- ance of boys and girls is not so easily distinguished. Nor can simple, general conclusions about boys' and girls' attainment be drawn from the data:

> Average figures for attainment conceal many differences between groups of pupils: some males achieve very high levels of attainment, and some females fail to achieve examination awards. Our research showed far greater differences in school experiences between high attainers and low attainers of both sexes and between those from advantaged and disadvantaged home backgrounds than between boys and girls. (Tinklin *et al.*, 2001, p. 2)

Thus Tinklin *et al.* (2001), while noting that there are broad gender trends, argue that there are other factors that can be as equally powerful in shaping the experiences of learners. We cannot then see gender as an isolated factor. Studies of patterns of attainment in and beyond Scotland point to the dangers of considering gender as disconnected from other aspects of pupil identities. Firstly, we will consider further the question of the significance of gender in education and then, secondly, explore the ways in which gender interacts with other social factors.

Approaches to gender in education

Historically, educational policy and practice was 'gender-blind': that is, the significance of gender in shaping the educational careers of boys and girls was either ignored or there was an unquestioned assumption that girls and women were not as intellectually able as boys and men. An example is the area of mathematics where boys and men were assumed to have a 'natural' ability and these assumptions underpinning the provision of education clearly acted to disadvantage girls and women. However such ideas were contested. Indeed as early as the 1790s, when the issue of female education was an area of public debate, Catherine Macaulay (1996) was arguing that the different progress of boys and girls in education was due to social circumstances rather that physical differences.

Despite the efforts both historically and within contemporary feminist discussions, deterministic assumptions about gender continue to circulate. An example is the annual debate in the press about the 'failure of boys', particularly when each year the publication of the national examinations results is a replaying of the traditional deterministic understanding of gender. Indeed as Arnot and Mac an Ghaill (2006, p. 1) argue these current debates 'simplistically suggest a new social order in which old gender hierarchies of industrial society have been inverted with women emerging as late modernity winners'. These discussions make unquestioned assumptions about what it means to be a woman/girl, man/boy – albeit the positions of these have reversed. However, such deterministic notions limit our efforts to develop a genuinely inclusive educational system. From the popular images it might be assumed that girls are all hardworking, obedient and succeeding at school, whereas boys are inevitably troublesome, disengaged and underperforming. We have to look for alternatives ways of viewing the issue of gender in education.

At a point where a significant number of women and girls are making advancements in education both as learners and as educational professionals, a solution might be to develop a 'gender-neutral' approach in which both girls and boys have equal access to the same high quality learning experiences. Any differences in outcomes would then be down to personal motivation or levels of ability. Indeed, in the dominant performance agenda this is the conventional wisdom underpinning many strategies to raise attainment: if we become more skilled in providing effective learning then the performance of all pupils will improve. However, such an approach overlooks the significance that gender plays in the educational experiences of girls and boys. Here we are facing a paradox: on the one hand, we should be concerned solely with learners but walk into any classroom and it is clear that we are dealing with 'boy learners' and 'girl learners'. Part of the paradox is that, at one level, gender should have little relevance: the fact that a learner in a classroom is a boy or is a girl should have no significance in determining aspiration, opportunity and achievement. At another level, gender is a core concept in an individual's identity from very early childhood and gender remains something very profound in our self-concept throughout our lives. This raises the question about what we mean by the concept of 'gender'.

The concept of 'gender'

There has been much discussion about the origins of the gender differences that are observed in education such as interest, friendship patterns, work habits and application, levels of achievement and attainment, better or poorer performances in specific subject areas within the curriculum. The different performance of girls and boys in the subject areas of language and mathematics are examples often cited. In language girls have tended to demonstrate greater linguistic skill at a much earlier age than boys and, in contrast, boys have tended to perform better in areas such as mathematics, technology and science. However, to pursue the issue of whether such differences are the result of the different physical make up of boys and of girls (including neurological differences) or whether these differences are the result of acculturation from a very early age has become a polarised debate that does not really help to move the issue of gender in educational policy and practice much further. In this search for the causes of these differences, there is always the danger of adopting a reductive stance in which assumptions are made about 'all girls' and 'all boys'. If we take the previous example of gender trends in language and mathematics, we know from our everyday experience as educators that some boys are highly skilled linguistically and some girls are highly skilled in areas such as mathematics and science and indeed some girls are progressing significantly in these areas. So these patterns cannot simply be a matter of genetics or physical differences. Yet there are broad trends in patterns of achievement, albeit these are changing, and so we have to consider the impact of acculturation on the achievement and learning of boys and girls. In other words, we need to consider how societal expectations of what it means to be a boy and what it means to be a girl are shaping the educational experiences and progress of pupils in school in Scotland. To consider this question we need to distinguish between the terms 'sex' and 'gender'.

Although the terms 'sex' and 'gender' are sometimes used interchangeably, as a result of feminist discussions (Oakley, 1972) a crucial distinction was made between these terms. Thus, 'sex' is used generally to refer to the biological differences of maleness and femaleness and 'gender' is used to refer to differences that have resulted from the process of socialisation. From a very early age girls learn what it means to be a girl – that is, to be feminine – from family, friends, the wider community and the mass media, as do boys who learn what it is to be masculine. However, this does not fully explain why there are differences between groups of girls and between groups of boys in their behaviour, interests and aspirations. We can point to a dominant ideal of femininity or masculinity within a particular society, what is termed 'hegemonic' masculinity or femininity that is recycled in exaggerated forms in images from popular culture. To take a simple but persistent example: contrast the images between the male athlete and the female model which continue to dominate as images in popular magazines where qualities of aggression and strength are emphasised for the former, and the physical beauty of the latter. We can also point to different masculinities and femininities: different ways of being a boy or a girl, the boy who does not like football, the athletic girl. These competing ideologies of masculinity and femininity become important when we consider gender intersecting with other social factors such as social class, race and ethnicity, disability and sexuality. The privileged form of masculinity or femininity can be determined by factors such as, for example, class, race or sexuality.

A distinction between 'sex' and 'gender', has been long established, but nevertheless there seems to be a continuing, almost unchangeable belief in the existence of a superordinate set of sex differences that define the right way of being a boy or a girl. Though this distinction between sex and gender has been crucial in challenging historical assumptions about the abilities of girls and of boys, there remains the unanswered question about the interaction between the biological and the social/cultural. The idea that there are significant sex differences remains a deeply ingrained idea in Western culture.

Much work has gone on over the last thirty years trying to map out the specific psychological differences between women and men. However, this is limited in two respects. Firstly, the evidence from research has revealed more similarities than differences. Indeed, the finding of sex similarity is the most common outcome of studies of psychological sex differences beginning with Maccoby and Jacklin's (1975) highly influential study, but as Squire (1989) and Connell (2002) both argue, these findings are not reported and do little to challenge the idea of two mutually exclusive gender roles. This, then, raises the question of the relationship between the body and culture. Although the attempt to distinguish between sex (biology) and gender (culture) has enabled us to begin to appreciate the impact of societal expectations, it has been difficult to determine what aspects of personality, behaviour or intellect are determined by biological difference and culture. Rather than try to keep a separation between sex and gender and try to determine which 'difference' is due to biological differences and which is due to acculturation, we have to understand the interaction between the body and the social. We often see 'sex' as the fundamental category upon which we lay the concept of 'gender'. We use the concepts of masculinity and femininity to make sense of and privilege specific attributes as more significant than others. However, Butler's (1990, 1993) groundbreaking work on gender highlights the way in which we give cultural and political sense to the sexed body because we already have the concept of gender that sets up two mutually exclusive categories. Connell (2002, p. 46) provides us with a useful notion 'social embodiment' to understand the relationship between body and society in which he argues that bodies are 'both agents and objects'. Further:

> Gender always involves social embodiment in this sense. Gender relations form a particular social structure, refer to particular features of bodies and form a circuit between them. Gender refers to the bodily structures and processes of human reproduction. These structures and processes do not constitute a 'biological base', a natural mechanism that has social effects. Rather they constitute an arena, a bodily site where something social happens. Among these things that happen is the creation of the cultural categories 'women' and 'men'...(Connell, 2002, p. 48)

Connell is drawing from the current philosophical explorations of the concept of 'gender' and though these discussions may seem distant from the material realities of daily life in the classroom, they serve to illustrate how powerful ideologies of gender as two mutually exclusive sets of attributes – femininity and masculinity – shape the experiences of children and young people in schools today. Therefore, we have to seek an approach to gender that appreciates some of the specific issues created by these ideologies of gender but at the same time not deploy such ideas in a deterministic way.

Masculinity and femininity

The idea of mutually exclusive categories continues to shape strategies adopted by schools for boys and for girls. For example, Martino and Berrill (2003) examining gender inequalities in relation to strategies to address boys' underachievement, critique New Right prescriptions for change to address the 'problems' of masculinity, particularly in schools. They argue such prescriptions are based upon assumptions about the 'natural' predisposition of boys which emphasise their tendency to behave, think and learn in particular ways (Martino and Berrill, 2003, p. 103). In a similar vein, Mac An Ghaill (1994, p. 8) criticises earlier strategies to address perceived discrimination against girls, pointing out that strategies such as changing school texts, establishing gender-fair teaching styles were well-intentioned, if naïve. He cites Arnot (1991, p. 453) in support of this case:

> The simplicity of the portrayal of the processes of learning and gender formation, its assumptions about the nature of stereotyping, its somewhat negative view of girls as victims had all contributed to the creation of particular school-based strategies.

These early attempts at developing gender strategies to address girls' achievement in school drew from a growing body of work in psychology, philosophy and politics which explored culture and gender. The work of

Gilligan (1982) in particular has been very influential in attempts to understand cultural differences between men and women. Gilligan postulated that the perceptions, values and conceptualisations of women were categorically different from those of men. From this work came important insights into the value-laden nature of the epistemologies and methodologies of the social sciences. However, work by Gilligan and others such as Baker Millar (1986) and Ruddick (1990) were based on an understanding of feminine and masculine as mutually exclusive and their position was to valorise femininity.

During the 1990s the distinction between masculinity and femininity was taken much further by a range of theorists such as Connell (2000), Epstein (1998) and Mac an Ghaill (1994) that has resulted in an understanding of the existence of femininities and masculinities. If we look at masculinity, Jackson (2002, p. 39) identifies four strands in the theorising of masculinities:

- Masculine identities are historically and culturally situated.
- Multiple masculinities exist.
- There are dominant and subordinate forms of masculinity.
- Masculinities are actively constructed in social settings.

Studies on gender such as these above have provided useful tools for analysing the causes of gender inequality. Academic work was found to be perceived by boys to be 'feminine' and therefore unattractive to those with hegemonic masculine identities. Academic achievement was not in itself seen to be demeaning, but being seen to work in school is noted as a problem for some boys. Jackson (2002) discusses how boys protect their self-worth in school settings where academic achievement is the single most important criterion in judging the worth of pupils. Caught between two competing influences on their sense of themselves – the need to conform to hegemonic masculinities and the desire to value one's own worth – Jackson outlines four strategies commonly employed by boys to protect their masculine identities in the face of pressure to work in school: procrastination, withdrawal of effort and rejection of academic work, avoidance of the appearance of work, and disruptive behaviour.

We can see parallel developments with the issue of girls and ideologies of femininity that operate to limit the educational experience of girls in school. Femininity is an equally complex concept as that of masculinity but there is an added dimension in that femininity signals a less powerful position and a less valued set of attributes. In other words, to be feminine is, within the dominant ideologies, to be less powerful and these contradictions shape the educational experiences of girls. Reay, (2001, p. 164) in her study of gender relations in a primary school in England, found these tensions evident in the behaviour and self-attitudes of the pupils:

The girls' struggle to make meaning of themselves as female constitutes a struggle in which gendered peer group hierarchies such as those in 3R [the class being observed] position boys as 'better' despite the mass of evidence to show they are neither as academically successful nor as well behaved as girls in the classroom. Peer group discourses constructed girls as harder working, more mature and more socially skilled. Yet, all the boys and a significant number of the girls, if not subscribing to the view that boys are better, adhered to the view that it is better being a boy. There are clearly confusions within gender work in this classroom. To talk of dominant femininity is to generate a contradiction in terms because it is dominant versions of femininity which subordinate the girls to the boys.

Nevertheless, it is important that we do not see boys and girl as simply passive but actively engage in the construction of gender in the classroom. As Houston (1994, p. 125) argues:

The *teacher* may well try to ignore gender, but the point is that the *students* are not ignoring it in their sense of how interactions should go and who is entitled to speak in the educational arena. Gender may be excluded as the *official* criterion, but it continues to function as an *unofficial* factor. (italics in the original)

A number of commentators take up the discussion of boys' classroom behaviour and the lengths to which they will go to appear not to be working. In this we can see an assertion of hegemonic forms of masculinity. Jackson (2002) noted the use of disruptive behaviour by boys to protect their masculine identities. As Jackson argues, disruptive behaviour can increase a boy's status with the peer group who may see him as demonstrating 'appropriate' forms of masculinity. Secondly, it can deflect attention away from academic performance and on to the behaviour. Thirdly, failure to achieve can be attributed to poor behaviour rather than to lack of ability and, fourthly, it may sabotage the academic efforts of classmates outwith the masculine hegemony. Thus, we can see how the dominant ideologies of masculinity work against boys' achievement. Further, as Archer and Yamashita (2003) argue, 'bad boy' masculinities are fun for those who espouse them, offering status, close friendships and enjoyment of life. It seems unlikely that the strategies adopted by schools offer as much to boys, nor will it be easy for schools to develop strategies that come close to addressing the complexities of boys' developing identities. Though hegemonic forms of masculinity are a powerful influence on attitudes and behaviour in school, we must also acknowledge that not all boys conform and some boys will actively seek alternative identities.

Similarly with girls, we can see the operation of hegemonic forms of femininity but in Reay's (2001, p.164) study discussed above, she found (some) girls were actively working against hegemonic forms of femininity that tie them to a powerless position:

> ... transgressive discourses and the deviant femininities they generate like Jodie's 'tomboys' and Debbie and Carly's espousal of 'girl power' accrue power in both the male and female peer group, and provide spaces for girls to escape gender subordination by the boys.

As well as offering an explanation for some of the gendered patterns in attainment, attitudes and behaviour, an understanding of the existence of dominant and transgressive forms of masculinity also support a critical appraisal of the strategies used by schools to address gender inequalities. Thus such strategies may be seen as underpinned by the misguided notion that masculinity is unidimensional, inherent and static. A parallel concern is evident in relation to girls. Though many girls exhibit desirable attributes such as being obedient, hardworking and conformist, there is a downside to such behaviours. Jones and Myhill (2004) illustrate the way in which the 'compliant girl' dominates teachers' understandings of gender and achievement and, where girls are perceived as underachieving, this is seen simply in terms of 'a lack of confidence' and issues of social disadvantage are not taken into account. Therefore, we need to consider the ideologies of gender that are implicit in strategies to address the learning needs of girls and of boys. Skelton (2001) criticises the widespread trend in schools and education authorities towards producing support materials designed to make classrooms more 'boy friendly' by endorsing one kind of masculinity – that which is aggressive, active and dominant. A similar criticism could be made if we assume that there is no problem with girls in education today.

Previously we considered the limitations of developing either a 'gender-blind' or a 'gender-neutral' approach in education as we have to recognise the powerful influence gender does have on boys' and girls' understanding of themselves as learners. At the same time we want to avoid a deterministic stance that narrows expectations and experiences of boys and girls. Houston (1994) proposes a third approach – a 'gender-sensitive' approach – which allows us to understand that the issue of gender is situational. Maher and Tetreault (1994, p. 226) take a similar stance in their discussion of developing pedagogies within co-educational classrooms that appreciate the dynamic nature of gender relations and the intersection of other social factors in placing individuals in less powerful or more powerful positions: 'Positional pedagogies could help them to explore those categories not as natural states, or as normal or abnormal conditions, but as different positions within a structural power dynamic.' Part of this dynamic is the intersection of gender with other social factors such as class, race, sexuality and disability.

Gender and other social factors

Archer and Yamashita (2003) argue for the need to recognise intersecting identities in policy and practice. By this account, gender interacts with other aspects of social being, for example, class, culture, ethnicity and sexuality, to create multiple forms of identity and ensuring that within the whole group of boys/girls and groups of boys/girls, for example, there are very different relationships to schools and schooling, depending on a range of other social factors. We will take two examples: the intersection of gender with race and gender with class. Mac an Ghaill (1988) deals with race and racism and shows how schools create alienation and disaffection in unintentional but potent ways. He also shows how the responses of black boys and black girls to institutional racism are different, with girls' responses characterised as 'resistance within accommodation' – compliance with formal and explicit rules whilst withholding any real engagement with the organisation. Boys, on the other hand, challenged directly the oppressive mechanisms they encountered and were more likely to be excluded.

If we look at the experiences of boys and of girls from working-class backgrounds we can see the intersection of class and gender shaping different educational experiences. The process of masculine, working-class identity construction is presented in the seminal study of Willis (1978) in which he describes the process through which a group of secondary-school 'lads' become increasingly resistant to school and explains this resistance in terms of their need to move into the culture which will shape their adult lives. Arnot (2003) reconsiders Willis's *work* in the light of contemporary research into social justice and identities and, notwithstanding valid criticisms, she argues for the continuing relevance of Willis's critique. Particularly this study provides insight into the 'lads' culture and demonstrated that forms of social class (anti-school) resistance are based on the celebration of traditional sexual identities. For working-class boys, engagement with the mental activity of school diminishes their sense of their masculinity, derived from their peer group, their family and their community. This theme of conflict between class/cultural affiliation and educational attainment is pursued by Reay (2002) in her discussion of Shaun's experience in a London 'sink' secondary school. Here, a poor working-class boy struggles, at some personal cost, to maintain his 'tough' status with his peer group whilst simultaneously aspiring to achieve at school.

One of the critical features about gender and social class is the high visibility of boys, but in contrast there is not a similar focus on the educational experiences of working class girls. In her study of the achievement of working-class girls in the education system, Plummer (2000) criticises the simplistic interpretation of statistics on the relative performances of boys and girls in national examinations in England. Within those overall statistics, it is argued, there is evidence that groups other than boys are faring badly. Plummer's concerns are that the widespread focus given to the supposed underachievement of boys has taken attention away from the continuing failure of the education system to provide equitably for other social, cultural and ethnic groups and, in particular, for working-class girls. Figures indicating the significant achievement of middle-class girls have been widely misinterpreted as indicative of a rise in the achievement of all girls. Given this intersection of gender and other social factors, there can be no one set of strategies that can be applied to all boys or all girls. Instead we need both to seek a variety of approaches and to ask critical questions about the underpinning ideas of gender that shape these policies and practices.

Addressing gender inequalities in Scottish schools

In this book we explore a range of strategies that have been developed to address gender inequalities in Scottish schools. To do so we draw from a SEED-funded research project (Condie *et al.*, 2005) which included a survey of local authorities and a number of case studies examining specific initiatives to tackle gender inequality in schools. In drawing from this material we take a critical stance and raise questions about the understandings of gender underpinning specific approaches. If strategies are based on polarised ideas of gender difference and an undiscerning development of 'boy-friendly' or 'girl-friendly' approaches, such strategies will only reinforce narrow definitions of what it means to be a boy or what it means to be a girl. Further, such strategies intended to enhance the educational prospects of boys and of girls may limit the capacity of schools to value and support the growth of other, and different, forms of gendered identity.

In the subsequent chapters we examine a range of strategies that have been developed in pre-5, primary and secondary schools to address gender inequalities. Some of these strategies are specifically targeted at groups of boys or groups of girls, others appreciate some of the different learning needs of both girls and boys and attempt to accommodate these within specific initiatives. In the case studies what comes across is a mixture of both ideals and pragmatism – that these strategies are about equality, fairness and social justice, at the same time they sit within the school's improvement programme to raise attainment. This brings with it not inconsiderable tensions and raise questions about the direction policy on gender and education should go in Scotland.

CHAPTER 2

RESPONDING TO CONCERNS: POLICIES AND STRATEGIES IN GENDER AND EDUCATION

Rae Condie

Introduction

Concern over gender-related inequalities, like many educational issues, has tended to wax and wane with time. In the mid 1970s and 1980s, concern was expressed over the lack of participation of girls in certain areas of the curriculum, notably the sciences and mathematics. More recently gender-related differences have come to the fore once again, but this time in relation to behaviour and, more significantly, attainment – areas where boys are now perceived as disadvantaged by aspects of schooling. This is not unique to the United Kingdom and similar concerns have been raised in, for example, Australia (Mills *et al.*, 2007) and Canada (Kehler and Greig, 2005). As part of the study of strategies implemented by Scottish schools to address such concerns, evidence of an underpinning rationale for their adoption, explicit and/or implicit, local and/or national, was sought in each case.

This chapter reflects on the role of policy in gender equality and education and considers how the issue of gender might be taken forward in the broader context of a policy framework for social justice and inclusion in education generally, as well as within the more focused area of learning and teaching. It draws together the evidence from the case studies in the SEED research project (Condie *et al.*, 2005) and the literature with the aim of identifying some of the common themes that have emerged in relation to the adoption of classroom strategies within pre-5 and school settings.

The policy context

In order to understand better the genesis and implementation of gender-related strategies in schools, it is necessary to consider the policy context in which they have arisen, at national and local levels. At the time of the study, there was no national policy that referred directly to gender-related dimensions of schooling. In recent years, the National Priorities have provided the broad framework for educational policy-making in Scotland (Scottish Executive, 2000). There are five priorities: Achievement and Attainment; Framework for Learning; Inclusion and Equality; Values and Citizenship; and Learning for Life. While, in the elaboration of these priorities, there is no specific reference to gender, the website (National Priorities, 2006) set up by the Scottish Executive to inform and support developments in schools provides a range of guidance and resources for schools. There are suggestions for staff development activities under the theme of 'gender' as well as linked contributions from teachers and researchers on the same topic. The series of eight activities under the gender theme reflect the issues that are to be explored in subsequent chapters. Examples include: 'It's cool for boys to write'; 'Separate the sexes in secondary schools?' and 'Gender differences from the earliest stages'. However there is no explicit overall organising structure for the resources on gender that might indicate a guiding philosophy or theoretical stance on the part of the Scottish Executive.

In the absence of an explicit or implicit national policy, evidence was sought by the project team regarding policy at local authority and/or school level. A brief questionnaire was sent to each local authority, asking whether or not any policy existed at authority level and what they expected of schools, either in terms of policy or practice. In addition, they were asked to provide examples of good practice of gender-related strategies in their schools if they were aware of any. Just over three-quarters of the 32 authorities responded and about half of these indicated that they had a policy that focused on gender. An analysis of the policy documents they subsequently supplied showed considerable variation in scope and detail. Many were 'corporate' policies that covered all aspects of the authority's activities, including employment and recruitment, with a smaller proportion concerned with educational provision and institutions. The latter tended to consist of statements of principle rather than provide guidance for day-to-day classroom practice.

When asked what the authority expected of schools with regard to a policy for gender, a typical response was: 'Not necessarily a stand-alone policy on gender but all schools have an equality policy.' In several instances, authorities reported that it was difficult to respond to gender-specific questions in the survey on the grounds that 'gender' was part of a more general inclusion policy and not dealt with explicitly. Authorities did acknowledge that gender might be an issue for schools to address, however. Just over half of those who responded expected to see gender issues on all school development and improvement plans, although others felt that it should only appear if there was evidence of a problem within that particular school. As with the nature of policies, gender-specific concerns were likely to be part of a broader theme. For example: 'Some schools will have specific strategies to tackle boys' underachievement, but this would be part of a whole school policy on raising attainment.'

Of the handful of policies that did make specific reference to gender, the focus tended to be on access to the curriculum, encouraging positive attitudes and countering stereotypes and prejudice. Three authorities recognised that gender was an issue in achievement but provided limited guidance. A fourth authority had published a support pack for schools which included a review of the literature and offered practical guidance on catering for the needs of boys and girls in order to raise achievement. It also stated that while the issue of boys' underachievement was important, the issue of equal opportunity for girls remained very relevant. Yet another authority provided no overall policy statement but sent documentation relating to the implementation of single-gender classes, including a brief review of the strategy by external consultants and achievement data from one secondary school that had implemented it. The data showed an improvement in the boys' performance levels and a narrowing of the gap between the boys and the girls.

One authority supplied three pieces of documentation – a general equal opportunities policy, a learning and teaching policy and a learning and teaching 'toolkit' designed to provide practical advice to teachers. The learning and teaching policy talked about inclusion, meeting the needs of the whole learner, multiple intelligences and learning styles, flexible curriculum structures and lifelong learners, although gender was not specifically mentioned. The statements were supported by references to expert views and research reports (e.g. Black *et al.*, 2002). The toolkit expanded on the policy statements and contained a significant section on gender, particularly boys' underachievement. Teachers were directed to a number of websites where they could find further information and advice, should they choose.

Thus the policy context varied significantly across authorities. In general, there was little documentation received from authorities regarding an overall policy for schools which explicitly referred to gender as either part of an inclusion agenda or as a stand-alone issue and even fewer had produced detailed guidance for teachers in schools. Most of the guidance that existed was concerned with raising achievement in general and for boys in particular.

Where opportunities for relevant staff development were offered, they were, in the main, concerned with gender-related differences in attainment and learning styles. While almost all authorities identified schools where gender-related strategies were in place in individual or groups of schools, often in the absence of any policy at authority level, there was little indication that these were directly supported or driven by staff development events, prior to or during their implementation.

In a few instances staff development was made available to support the implementation of strategies to raise attainment. Staff in several of the schools visited had attended seminars and workshops on themes such as learning styles that included discussion of gender as a pertinent factor. In the main, these had been delivered by external consultants and their practical advice had been valued and adopted in various ways. Some of those interviewed had followed up the sessions with personal research, were knowledgeable about some of the key literature and were working to address issues within their own classroom or institution, guided by what they had learned. For the majority, gender was addressed within the context of broader themes such as exclusion, pupil support and class organisation.

In sum, while most authorities were able to point to schools that had adopted strategies designed to address specific gender-related concerns, very few of these existed within a framework of policy statements, staff development activities or strategic initiatives at national, authority or school level. In a few instances, the strategies observed within individual schools were coordinated, often loosely, by the local authority to address a specific concern such as literacy or self-esteem, with schools developing their own strategies in response.

Views on gender as an issue in schooling

Given the lack of a clear, explicit policy context in which to situate the strategies encountered, it was necessary to determine how important teachers, pupils and parents considered gender to be in determining success in school and to explore how their views had been shaped.

Most teachers believed that gender was a pertinent issue in the context of schooling although, for many, gender was but one of a complex cluster of factors which included social background, ethnicity and culture. While some were actively working to address gender-related issues of achievement, access or choice, a small minority of teachers were of the view that 'gender' had been addressed in the 1980s and 1990s and was no longer an issue.

Pupils were aware that gender played a role in the nature of their school experiences and readily identified a number of generally accepted aspects of being a boy or a girl in the classroom. Girls thought that boys got more attention and both boys and girls agreed that girls were better learners. Even amongst the youngest children who contributed to the case studies, there was evidence of stereotypical views of what constituted appropriate activities for 'boys' or 'girls' in school or in later life, although it was noted that some children were prepared to challenge these stereotypes and break down some of the associated barriers.

Parents tended to think that gender was not as important as achievement – 'being a boy or a girl, doesn't matter, it's how clever they are' – and most failed to see any link between the two. They were aware of the widely reported underachievement of boys, particularly in reading, but were rarely aware of any specific strategies to address gender inequalities operating within the school. What they wanted, broadly speaking, was a 'good school', one where the overall ethos was positive. Parents tended to be more aware of, and involved in, gender-related strategies in the pre-5 and primary sectors than in the secondary, with achievement and behaviour the key issues. An understanding of the ways in which gender could influence the pupil experience and, potentially, result in long term advantage and dis-advantage within the school system was patchy.

Where there was evidence of awareness and even concern amongst teachers, there was also evidence of uncertainty as to the best ways to deal with the inequities identified. In practice, the strategies observed were a combination of activities aimed at addressing boy-specific concerns, such as literacy, and the adoption of broad inclusive approaches to education, where the emphasis was on *all* pupils attaining in line with their capabili-ties. Where strategies were targeted at specific 'problem' areas, they were often adopted as local solutions to more widespread concerns and focused variously on literacy, behaviour and attainment, usually with boys as the target group.

It was clear that some of the concern had been driven by the moral panic engendered by media statements and reports on 'failing boys', par-ticularly in literacy. These have come to occupy the vacuum that has been created by a lack of a strong central policy commitment, even serving as de facto policies at school level. Lingard (2003) observed a similar phe-nomenon in Australia where management responsibility and accountability have been increasingly devolved to schools, accompanied by a reduction in central direction and policy formation. As a result, schools have become more active in policy-making and strategic planning in line with the greater degree of self-determination afforded to schools and school-based manage-ment practices.

Gender inequality has been one of the areas addressed in this way. In a survey of 100 state school principals, Lingard found that more than half saw boys as the new disadvantaged on the basis of, primarily, achievement evidence (Lingard *et al.*, 2000). As in the UK, schools developed local policies on gender and initiated a range of strategies including the greater involvement of fathers, all-boys classes and an emphasis on boys' levels of literacy.

The strategies introduced in Scottish schools aim to address similar topics. Robust research evidence (as opposed to statistical data) and academic theory have so far played a minor and somewhat inconsistent role in driving practice. An analysis of the strategies and their implementation provides some clues as to the underpinning assumptions made about boys and girls and schooling by those involved. In the study of Scottish schools described here, there was evidence of a tendency to perceive boys and girls as essentially two separate groups, each fairly homogeneous. Stated simply, the assumption is that all boys share certain characteristics and respond in similar ways to the demands and expectations of schools while all girls share different characteristics, resulting in different responses. In several instances there was a polarisation of what it meant to 'be a boy' and 'be a girl' based on definitions of masculinity and femininity that drew on the traditional stereotypes of the well-behaved, compliant girl and the active, more challenging boy. However the 'all girls'/ 'all boys' distinction does not bear scrutiny.

All boys and all girls?

There is well-documented evidence that overall, boys and girls can and do vary in some characteristics but this does not mean that all boys share the same characteristics, nor all girls. Gray and Mclellan (2006) investigated primary pupils' attitudes to school with the aim of identifying the extent of gender-related differences. Overall, they concluded that the girls were consistently more positively disposed to school than were the boys in their study, particularly with regard to engagement in schooling and behaviour; although boys scored higher on academic self-esteem.

Further analysis of the data indicated that the situation was more complex. Five clusters of attitudes were identified, described as: enthusiastic and confident; moderately interested but easily bored; committed but lacking self-esteem; socially engaged but disaffected; alienated. While boys featured in significantly greater numbers in the 'alienated' and 'disaffected' groups, and girls were in the majority with regard to 'confident and successful', there were boys and girls in each of the groups and none was exclusively male or female. The composition of most clusters was therefore gendered, to a greater or lesser extent, although both sexes were represented in each cluster. When the emphasis is on differences between the sexes, as in reports on achievement and behaviour, it is easy to overlook the extent to which boys and girls demonstrate considerable similarities across a range of characteristics such as attitudes, abilities, dispositions and behaviours. Gray and Mclellan highlight the potential danger in taking approaches to school improvement that are based on a narrowly gendered view of pupil characteristics, particularly one that is based stereotypical conceptions of masculinity and femininity.

Mills *et al.* (2007) similarly warn against initiatives based on essentialised differences between boys and girls. Reflecting on an Australian Parliamentary report on gender in education, they note that much of the argument therein is based on the premise that boys are a disadvantaged group and that action is required to address the resultant inequity. They argue that the responses made by schools to data that show superior attainment levels for girls have been, in large part, media-driven. A lack of government direction based on research and analysis has allowed a common-sense understanding of gender differences to drive practice, neglecting the complex ways in which social variables such as social class, ethnicity and family background interact in determining the individual boy's or girl's experience of school.

One of the theories used to support the recommendations for learning and teaching made in the Australian report, and which was frequently mentioned by Scottish teachers, is that of gender-related learning styles. In the Scottish study, the strategies adopted were often justified in terms of boys and girls having different preferred learning styles. Several teachers had attended seminars and other staff development events that involved advice on learning styles and gender-related differences.

Learning style theories generally hold that an individual's preferred learning style has a physiological basis and is fairly fixed for the individual – 'characteristic cognitive, affective and physiological behaviours that serve as relatively stable indicators of how learners perceive, interact with and respond to the learning environment' (Keefe, 1979, p. 4). There is a significant body of literature that investigates and explores the identification and classification of learning styles and how they might influence the learning process (see, for example, Riding and Rayner, 1998; Kolb, 1984; Coffield *et al.*, 2004), and a number of instruments have been developed to identify individual learning styles (e.g. Felder and Silverman, 1988; Felder and Soloman, 1999). Felder and Soloman (1999) add a cautionary note, however, advising that a profile of an individual's learning style only provides a pointer to the probability of a tendency towards particular learning experiences or instructional styles. They warn that it does not provide a reliable assessment of a learner's suitability for particular subjects or approaches and that labelling learners in this way may be misleading, even damaging. When learning styles are discussed in relation to gender-specific strategies, as in the Australian report or in the Scottish study, the term is rarely portrayed as problematic or subject to the limitations outlined above.

The attribution of preferences in learning styles or other characteristics to 'being a boy' or 'being a girl' is based on biological determinism which neglects the impact of socialisation within the home, community, school or wider culture. Mills *et al.* (2007) noted that the research evidence used to support the recommendations in the Australian report was of this kind – relatively limited and based on a fairly simplistic view of natural dispositions towards learning resulting from biological differences. There are dangers inherent in adopting a strong stereotypical identity based on biological determinants as the model of the male pupil when selecting resources, teaching styles and reward systems.

Strategies that are based on such a model are typified by contexts traditionally associated with boys (action adventures, technology and sport), by requiring short concentration spans and frequent change of pace. While this may be effective in managing those boys who conform or aspire to such the hegemonic masculinity, it ignores, if not disadvantages further, those boys who do not. Nor does it address the issue of whether this is an appropriate, accurate or even helpful image to promote in schools, either for girls or for the wider community.

Lingard (2003) sets current concerns about boys as disadvantaged against the historical background of feminist ideology and politics and the policies of the 1970s and 1980s which saw girls as disadvantaged. He argues that the strength of current concerns is in part due to a broader backlash against feminism which began in the early 1990s and has influenced recent policy-making, resulting in a defensive and recuperative masculine stance. Two reports, he argues, have been significant in influencing the nature and direction of gender-related policy in Australia. One was a study of boys and literacy while the other focused on differences in initial post-school destinations for males and females: both analyses concluded that boys were disadvantaged in school. Lingard challenges the interpretation of the data, noting that a more nuanced reading indicates that not all boys are disadvantaged and other factors are at play, such as socio-economic status. Reinforcing this, *Interchange* 70 on 'Gender and pupil performance' makes it clear that gender is a significant factor but states that 'social background is a greater source of inequality and underachievement than gender' (SEED, 2001)

The recuperative approach also calls for more male teachers in schools to counter the lack of male role models and the 'girl-friendly' culture of schooling (Kehler and Greig, 2005; Mills *et al.*, 2007). The lack of male role models in secondary schools in particular has been raised as an issue in Scotland (see news.bbc.co.uk/1/hi/scotland/3087880.stm) and recent statistics from the Executive confirm that most teachers in Scottish primary and secondary schools are female, with figures of 92% and 59% respectively. In addition, trend figures for recent years show a slight decline in the numbers of male teachers, overall and in promoted posts (Scottish Executive, 2007b).

The argument for more male teachers to provide models of masculinity for boys draws heavily on sex role socialisation theory, either explicitly or implicitly (Mills *et al.*, 2007). Where there are few male role models, it is argued, boys will identify with those that are available and these will tend to be the macho, hetero-normative masculinities of the media. As a result, they will fail to develop appropriate interpersonal skills, including emotional sensitivity and communication abilities. Such a stance fails to account for the differences within and across groups of men and underestimates the extent to which our culture remains heavily masculine in terms of power and reward and pervades children's experiences both in and out of school. Which exerts the greater influence on learning what it is to be male – the macho stereotypes valorised by the media or the absence of male teachers in the classroom?

A better balance of male and female teachers is desirable on grounds of equity alone. It has been argued that there are multiple masculinities and more men working with boys can provide opportunities to challenge narrow and restrictive constructions of being male (Riddell *et al.*, 2005; Mills *et al.*, 2007). However, Kehler and Greig (2005) and Mills *et al.* (2007) are concerned that some advocates of increasing the percentages of male teachers hold to a model of the male teacher that conforms to the hegemonic masculinity, citing arguments that, for example, men are better than women at controlling pupils.

Sustainable strategies and long-term impact

Not all authorities or schools saw a need for strategies to address gender inequalities and many of those observed in Scottish schools tended to be partial, varied and frequently lacking a conceptual or operational framework that included a rigorous evaluation of their impact. It seems unlikely that such a situation will address adequately the gender inequalities reflected in the data, for both boys and girls.

The introduction of the Gender Equality Duty (GED), however, should prompt a major review of policy and practice in education as well as in other areas of public life. The GED, Scotland, came into force in April 2007 (Equal Opportunities Commission, 2007). It requires public authorities to promote gender equality and eliminate sex discrimination and identifies both general and specific duties that they must address. The general duty has two strands: the elimination of unlawful discrimination and harassment, and the promotion of equality of opportunity for men and women. The specific duty requires authorities to gather information and data regarding the impact on men and women, boys and girls of policies and practices, to assess their impact, to identify priorities, to set gender equality objectives and to take action to achieve these. Each authority must publish a gender equality scheme, report annually on progress and review progress on a three-yearly basis.

The guidance for pre-16 education providers in Scotland expects each education authority to publish its own gender equality scheme which covers policies and practices in schools. It highlights a number of significant gender-related inequalities in Scottish schools, specifically girls outperforming boys, higher school exclusion rates for boys, gender preferences for subjects and work experience choices. It also identifies a number of challenges: attracting more men into childcare and teaching roles; properly rewarding and promoting women in the school sector (where there is an imbalance in favour of men in posts of responsibility); and enhancing the status of and value placed on, for example, nursery nurses and classroom assistants (roles normally regarded as caring, quasi-domestic and, essentially, 'women's work').

The Equal Opportunities Commission (EOC) argues that gender equality schemes can be embedded within the various programmes and initiatives already in place to improve and enhance the educational experience of pupils, such as Ambitious Excellent Schools and a Curriculum for Excellence. The need to address the requirements of the GED provides an opportunity for schools to review their approaches to gender (in)equality and identify opportunities to mainstream gender equality within existing improvement initiatives.

The requirements of the GED are likely to lead to an increase in the number and kind of gender-related initiatives in schools and across authorities. However, the GED in itself is unlikely to change the situation significantly. The review of gender strategies implemented by Scottish schools indicates that just looking to the implementation of a series of discrete strategies may be problematic as a result of the partial understanding of the issues. In addition, the Guidance from the EOC tends to talk in terms of 'all boys' and 'all girls' rather than a more nuanced interpretation of the issues raised, thus reinforcing the polarised views encountered and providing a potential impediment to effective gender equality schemes.

In reviewing a number of large-scale initiatives, Fullan (2005) identified several features that contributed to their effective implementation including: the acknowledgement of poor performance and the need to seek solutions; a focus on improving practice and achievement; the development of a system-wide framework and infrastructure to support innovation and change; distributed leadership (so that sustainability is not dependent on a lone 'champion'); the availability of relevant, useful professional development; and the recognition that change takes time, particularly where significant culture change is involved.

These characteristics reflect two key building-blocks for change – capacity building and accountability. Capacity building requires a programme of staff development opportunities to support the acquisition and development of the requisite skills, understanding and attitudes to bring about the desired change. Determining impact and demonstrating change (accountability) demands systematic data gathering, monitoring and evaluation procedures as integral components of any initiative. While Fullan's analysis was based on studies of large-scale, often national developments, these characteristics have considerable relevance for school-level strategies to address gender-related differences.

There is already evidence in Scotland to support this model of change management. The Scottish Executive's Assessment is for Learning (AifL) initiative, based on a programme of capacity building alongside monitoring and evaluation, has been effective in securing change in assessment practices in schools (Condie *et al.*, 2005). (It should be acknowledged that schools also received considerable financial support from the Scottish Executive – a significant factor in the early stages.)

Most of the gender-related strategies observed in Scottish schools showed some of the characteristics listed, but few if any, possessed all of them. The first, the awareness that things were not as they should be, or could be, was evident in all instances – as was the second. All case study schools and authorities were aware of and concerned by gender-related differences in performance levels, behaviour statistics (e.g. exclusion rates) and/or subject choices. A decision had been taken, at some level, to introduce changes to structures and/or practices as whole school or stage-specific initiatives to address these differences.

A third characteristic identified as instrumental in achieving sustained change was the development of a system-wide framework and infrastructure. This was witnessed only in a limited way in the 'bags of books' or 'story sacks' strategies which had developed from a national initiative to improve literacy – the National Year of Reading in 1998 (Scottish Office, 1998). While some resources were made available, the focus was on literacy generally rather than boys in particular and there was limited monitoring or evaluation of the outcomes. Other strategies lacked coherence or were inconsistently implemented. For example, one strategy to promote positive behaviour involved a reward system which some pupils perceived to be inconsistently applied by teachers, diminishing its impact.

There was evidence of effective, distributed leadership in some of the strategies. In one authority-driven initiative to raise self-esteem and confidence in pre-5 and early primary pupils, ownership of some elements was handed over to participants once established. There was a clear need to feel involved, valued and in control of some aspect of the strategy if it was to attract genuine commitment from participants.

For change to be effective, teachers need to operate from a position of informed professional judgement (Barber, 2002). While many of those interviewed made reference to educational consultants, researchers and theorists, this was rarely as the result of targeted staff development events on gender-related differences and their implications for learning and teaching. Where change was observed this was often driven by individual teachers' own interests or experiences, but were not always underpinned by a deeper understanding of the issues. This has implications for the scalability and transferability of strategies at anything other than a superficial level.

The literature indicates that gender, and its impact on performance, behaviour and life chances, is complex and multi-dimensional. In addition, it intersects with other factors to the extent that simple one-dimensional strategies are rarely effective. Change takes time, especially where the aim is to change deeply entrenched attitudes and culturally determined patterns of behaviour. The evidence that there are gender-related differences in the ways that boys and girls experience and benefit from schooling is compelling – addressing these inequalities requires coherent, inclusive policies and gender-sensitive practices to be developed and sustained throughout the educational careers of children and young people.

When new initiatives are introduced as a response to a 'problem', as in the strategies observed in Scottish schools, there is a need to monitor the impact, to determine if they are making a difference. Some schools used assessment data (from national testing or external certification) to measure change, but in many instances teachers' subjective perceptions were the only evidence provided. In the following chapters we will explore some of the strategies being adopted in the area of behaviour, literacy and the organisation of learning and consider critically the implications of these for policy and practice in the area of gender and education.

CHAPTER 3

LITERACY AND GENDER
– CONTEXTUALISATION AND DEVELOPMENT

Alastair McPhee

Introduction

One of the areas of concern with policy and practice in education is the question of literacy. Literacy is regarded as essential, acting as a gateway to the curriculum and achievement. Literacy has also taken on a wider significance in terms of social and political development most notably through the work of Paolo Friere where literacy is the means to enable disempowered groups to develop agency and tackle issues of poverty and social marginalisation. However, trends in education indicate that literacy is gendered, with greater numbers of boys than girls not achieving in language. In Scotland there has been a long tradition in developing literacy across all sectors of society as the basis for the development of a school education system nationally.

In this chapter we look back to these historical antecedents in the development of literacy in education in Scotland to illustrate the central place the development of literacy has in the educational process. Given the importance of literacy, we then consider the way in which literacy has become a key issue in discussions about gender in education, particularly the progress of boys. It is against this backdrop that specific strategies used by schools are explored. Literacy is capable of multiple definitions: for example, it may be defined as simply the ability to decode text and to understand the representation of sound in orthography. On the other hand, it might also be defined as a higher-order skill in which it is used metacognitively in order to access concepts and understandings, or to attain creative expression. Ultimately, literacy may be seen as a means of advancing democracy and empowerment. For the purposes of at least the first part of this chapter, we shall be looking at the definition of literacy as the acquisition of basic reading skills.

The development of literacy in Scottish schools

These skills have long been a concern in Scottish education – and indeed in the education systems of other nations. For instance, Ornstein and Levine talk of the 'essentialist' curriculum in the American school (Ornstein and Levine, 1994, p. 526). If the development is traced, we can go back as far as the end of the fifteenth century, where each main town in Scotland had at the least, a burgh school (Hunter, 1972, p. 2). The early development of skills of reading and writing were, of course, related largely to concerns of the church and the accessibility of Holy Scripture and the liturgy, and the teaching of Latin was undertaken in many establishments as a means to this end.

The Reformers of the sixteenth century proposed an articulated system of education which would develop from elementary to higher education, and through which a godly society would be created. (Hunter, 1972; Anderson, 2003). Although this commendable initiative was not enacted at the time, by the end of the seventeenth century a network of parish schools had been established in the Lowlands, though most certainly not in the Highlands. Elementary schooling did not become compulsory until the 1872 Act was passed: in 1855, male literacy in the Lowlands was estimated at 89% for men and 77% for women (Houston, 1985). In the Highlands and Islands the promotion of literacy in English as opposed to that in Gaelic was a feature (Paterson, 2003, p. 49), although some teaching in the early stages was still done in Gaelic. The gender gap was closed in the succeeding years up until 1900, when it was effectively closed, although there remained a 1% difference in favour of males. The twentieth century has seen a strong movement towards an integrated system of education, ultimately culminating in the organisation of secondary education along the familiar comprehensive lines which we know today.

Concern for literacy has always been a feature of Scottish schooling, and that concern has remained strong. Within the last sixty years, it has featured in a large number of curricular documents. For instance, the 1950 Primary Memorandum (SED, 1950) discusses literacy and the teaching of English language not only in terms of the fostering of the ability to read, but also in terms of the ability to express oneself creatively in speech and writing (SED, 1950, paragraphs 164 and 165). This need for expression features widely in the 1965 Primary Memorandum, which is widely seen as a landmark document in the liberalisation process in Scottish education. Here, literacy is enshrined as a means of accessing knowledge but also as part of the Language Arts and as an expressive medium (SED, 1965). Although some parts of the 'learning to read' section, with the stress on phonics highlight a continuity with an older, more traditional form of education which by that time had become firmly embedded in Scottish society, the document is notable for a multi-modal approach which differs little from thinking at the commencement of the twenty-first century. Subsequent curricular documentation (e.g. Consultative Committee on the Curriculum (CCC), 1983; 1986) reinforced this multi- modal approach rather than modified it. In 1991, the National Guidelines for English Language 5–14 were published (Scottish Office Education Department (SOED), 1991), and the strands which were advocated again were based on a multi-modal model, albeit one which included knowledge about language in order to meet political pressure. It is most interesting to note that many of the concerns which were articulated in the 10–14 document of 1986 are currently (2006) being re-visited in the Curriculum for Excellence initiative. Such concerns include the de-cluttering of the curriculum, rebalancing it, and the concept of the child as successful learner.

One last feature of the development of literacy in Scottish schools has been the ability of the relevant policy communities in Scotland to be responsive to UK national initiatives – but at the same time, to develop these in peculiarly Scottish ways. Thus, one can trace, for instance, the influence of the Bullock Report (DES, 1975) in the development of the teaching of English language. However, while these policy communities were aware of the existence of Cox and Kingman – two documents which were very influential south of the border – they nonetheless chose to take from them what they felt was useful in the Scottish context rather than to allow the process of policy formation in language and literacy skills to be unduly influenced by them (McPhee, 1996). Thus literacy in Scotland, since the middle of the twentieth century, has been seen as not only a gaining of the basic skills but also as a means to self-expression and communication.

The third area in which literacy may be seen as an essential skill is in the empowerment of individuals and of disadvantaged groups in society. A number of thinkers have advocated this: Dewey, for example, saw education as essential in the achievement of a truly democratic state. In more recent years, Paolo Freire has argued that education has a liberating quality and that indeed, it is essentially a political act. Firstly in *Pedagogy of the Oppressed* (Freire, 1970) and later in works such as *Pedagogy of Hope: Reliving Pedagogy of the Oppressed* (Freire, 1994), he deconstructs education and language in a manner which sees them as formative in the achievement of both freedom and dominance. What is sure is that in Scotland at least, education has been a powerful agent of social change and whether or not Freirian ideas have driven this, the effect of education – particularly in the last one hundred and thirty years or so – has been unarguable (Paterson, 2003).

Literacy as a gendered issue

In one sense, literacy has always been at the heart of debates on gender. The decisions taken in the past to prioritise the education of boys over that of girls and the restricted curricula offered to generations of girls and women in the past bear ample testimony to that fact. Even the aims of education for females have been directed towards fitting them for subservient roles: as recently as the 1950s 'housewifery' remained a subject wholly reserved for girls. In higher education, for instance, it was only in 1889 following the passing of the Universities (Scotland) Act that that women were allowed to graduate from the University of Glasgow, although they had been allowed to attend classes for some time previously (Glasgow University, 2006). Such classes were restricted to the daughters of those who could afford the fees, of course, and were in no sense widely accessible.

In more recent years, literacy concerns have centred around perceptions of underachievement by boys. In Scotland, the present situation is that boys' achievement in reading and writing at all ages is surpassed by that of girls as the 2005 Scottish Survey of Achievement in English language and core skills noted: 'girls performed consistently better than boys in reading. This difference was statistically significant at P3 and P5. By P7 although girls still performed better than boys, the difference was no longer significant and by S2 there was no consistent difference between boys and girls' (Condie *et al.*, 2005, p. 5). In addition, teachers rated girls more highly in terms of their reading attainment than they rated boys. Where writing is concerned, 'Gender differences in level profiles for writing were statistically significant at all four stages, with teachers rating girls' writing more highly than boys' writing and more girls than boys achieving higher levels (Condie *et al.*, 2005, p. 7).

The position in Scotland where literacy is concerned, is *apparently* quite clear. From a situation where female attainment was circumscribed by limitations in social and professional horizons and where schooling and education was calibrated for girls in terms of fulfilling these limited roles, female attainment is now superior to that of the male. Nor is this, seemingly, a recent phenomenon. Analyses of data similar to the above have concluded that average levels of attainment for boys are lower than for girls at all stages and across almost all areas of the Scottish curriculum (Forde *et al.*, 2005).

The issue of boys and literacy has been the subject of investigation on an international basis. In England, Strand (1997) carried out an analysis of the attainment of pupils in schools in Wandsworth, London based on baseline assessment in reception class through to Key Stage 1 of the National Curriculum. The results showed that girls made more progress than boys during this stage, although social and cultural factors also played a big part in determining success, as well as the quality of the schooling itself.

However, it is dangerous to look at statistics relating to achievement by gender in isolation. Rather, it is necessary to realise that other factors such as social class and ethnicity also exert a powerful influence. Gender cannot be considered apart from these other influences on pupil identity (Gorard, 2001; Tinklin, 2003; Croxford *et al.*, 2003). From these studies it is clear that some working-class girls do badly, while some middle-class boys do very well, and that analysis has to take account of many wider cultural factors. Gorard *et al.* (2001) find that in terms of aggregate scores such as government benchmarks, the gap between boys and girls in Wales is actually decreasing, although girls have the advantage in English language with an increasing gender gap as school careers progress. Solsken (1993) reinforces the concept of children in the US constructing gendered identities through interaction with families and peers, and stresses the role which family interaction plays in this process. Alloway and Gilbert (1997) examine the complex nature of the issue in Australia, and identify ways in which the construction of literacy in schools runs counter to the dominant constructions of masculinity in society: they advocate an approach which works with social constructions of masculinity and see a need to provide strategies which will accommodate the reform agenda for the progress of girls as well.

A major work which has been undertaken with regard to gendered achievement is that by Younger and Warrington (2004) for the Department for Education and Skills in England. This study looked not only at the causes of gendered achievement, but also at ways in which the 'gender gap' might be addressed. They, too, found that achievement levels as measured by national tests are rising through time, and that this has had the effect of widening the 'gap' in some schools and local education authorities. Achievement by girls has exceeded that by boys (although both genders have improved) and the gap once established, has become stable. However, they too find, as did Tinklin *et al.* (2001) and Croxford *et al.* (2003), that many boys continue to achieve at a high level, while there are other girls who under-achieve. However, they find that the greatest concern is in English, where at Key Stage 2, fewer than 80% of boys achieve at the same level as girls, and at Key Stage 4 where girls have improved in mathematics and science – and this has not been matched by a comparable improvement by boys in English and the humanities.

It may therefore be assumed – with due regard to context and situation – that in general terms, achievement by boys in areas associated with literacy has not matched that of girls in recent years. This phenomenon is seen by some as having caused a 'moral panic' (Frosh *et al.*, 2003) as noted in Chapter 1 above. (It may be appropriate to reflect that for hundreds of years, underachievement by girls has not caused such a panic to occur.) Additionally, this 'crisis' has become a concern for politicians: Peter Peacock, the then Education Minister in the devolved Scottish government, accepts that it is 'one of the major challenges facing the education system'. He further accepts that Scotland is not alone in facing the challenge and that it is 'an issue which is common across the Western world' (Denholm, 2006).

There have been a number of explanations offered for this underachievement. It has been suggested that developmental factors may inhibit the development of the language centres in the brain in some males (e.g. Byrnes, 2001, pp. 136–7). However, most commentators seem to feel that this biological explanation is less likely to hold good when compared to the social and cultural factors which affect development. Murphy and Elwood (1999), for instance, suggest that boys and girls experience the curriculum in different ways and that they respond in different ways to their experiences of schooling and society. Noble and Bradford (2000) debate the nature of the 'crisis' of underachievement by boys in social, political and educational terms and suggest potential strategies for dealing with it, whereas Francis (2000) suggests that the ways in which both boys and girls construct their identities are important, and argues that gender should not be seen in oppositional terms. Likewise, Myhill (2002) suggests that the current tendency to construct underachievement in terms of gender is not helpful and that aspects of pedagogy and social interaction in classroom situations are more relevant to explain underachievement. The role of teachers has been discussed by many commentators: for instance, it has been argued that the gender of the teacher is important in the provision of appropriate role models. Boys, it is argued, should have access to male teachers in a heavily feminised teaching profession, and particularly where they do not have male carers at home (e.g. Tinklin *et al.*, 2001, p. 110). However, Carrington *et al.* (2005) in an empirical study suggest that role modelling is a relatively insignificant when compared to other teacher traits. This scepticism concerning the importance of role modelling is borne out in other studies, too (e.g. Kenway *et al.*, 1998; Carrington and Skelton, 2003).

To summarise, then, historical factors suggest that a gendered view of literacy of one sort or another has been in place for some time. In more recent years the concept of literacy as a gendered issue has evolved due to the apparent underachievement by boys compared to girls in measures of attainment concerned with language and skills such as reading and writing: it has been suggested that this has caused a 'moral panic' or a 'crisis' and that an apparent 'gender gap' has been created. As we discussed in the first chapter, several explanations have been offered for this phenomenon. It has been suggested, for instance, that there are possible biological explanations, but it is more likely that social and cultural factors are responsible. The role of schools, of pedagogy and the teachers themselves in the creation of this phenomenon has also been investigated and there has been debate as to whether the provision of appropriate role models in a feminised profession and a society where child care is becoming more and more the province of women is effective in combating the apparent underachievement by boys. The next section of this chapter will look at some initiatives which have been put in place in Scotland, and will critically appraise these in terms of their effectiveness.

Strategies employed in Scottish schools to address literacy issues in boys

This section of the chapter addresses strategies which have been put in place in schools in Scotland to address literacy concerns with respect to boys, which have been highlighted earlier. In doing this, it draws upon the resources and fieldwork of the studies which led to the publication of *Strategies to Address Gender Inequalities in Scottish Schools* (Condie *et al.*, 2005). There is no suggestion that the section is exhaustive or even comprehensive in nature: rather, it deals with case studies of professional practice in the literacy field and locates these case studies in their proper contexts, both social and educational. The section is divided into three subsections: early years, primary schools and secondary schools, including transition strategies.

Early years' strategies

Early years' literacy is tackled in both pre-5 and primary schools. In these sectors, a number of strategies have been suggested as representing good practice. Some strategies are intended to improve literacy generally, but within these can be embedded a positive drive to engage boys with literacy. The schools which were concerned in the SEED study (Condie *et al.*, 2005) were located in both rural and urban contexts and drew their pupils from a wide variety of social contexts: this was confirmed by reference to the Scottish Area Deprivation Index, which maps deprivation in various contexts by postcode. The initiatives were, in some instances, developed in response to, and supported by, the Scottish Executive's Read Together campaign to develop and encourage home reading. This campaign is in turn, supported by a website Read Together which catalogues good practice in reading across Scotland so that it might be shared more widely (Read Together, 2006). Prominent in the strategies which are suggested by the Executive's *Home Reading Initiative*, and which feature in the section of the website devoted to local developments, are techniques involving story sacks or bags. These were observed in use during the study, and were supported either by a grant from the local authority or by the Scottish Executive.

The principle of the story sack or bag is that parents and children are engaged in the reading activity together, and that reading is seen to be a pleasurable encounter. Sacks contain a book, related games, sometimes a toy and sometimes also suggestions or tasks for further activity. The sacks are often made up by the children themselves, who choose the materials, and are always taken home. At home, the parent(s) and the child take part in the activities together, including the reading. The presence of the toy or game acts as a motivator, in that the family then associate reading with enjoyment together. In the case study schools in the 2005 research, the story sacks were part of a wider strategy to improve the language skills of all pupils which had become embedded over some years, but were thought to be particularly valuable for boys. It is perhaps relevant to state that none of the schools experienced serious underachievement from boys, even though their social backgrounds were very mixed (Condie *et al.*, 2005, p. 25). Schools stated that the strategy was effective, and that the attitudes of the boys towards books had improved and become more positive over time. When discussion was held with the pupils, they reacted very positively to the strategy, looking forward to taking the sacks home. Sometimes they were able to make suggestions for the development of the contents. While they were aware that the idea was to encourage them to read, there was no awareness of any gender dimension. There was strong parental support for these initiatives, and a feeling that they were of considerable benefit to the children. Some staff development had occurred in the case study schools, but there was little evidence of a joined up national approach such as would be suggested in the term 'national literacy strategy'; nonetheless, it is clear from the evidence of the Read Together website, that the story sacks are widely implemented in early literacy strategies. In the use of this set of strategies, in some circumstances it seems that there is an awareness – at least on the part of teachers – of the gender issues in relation to early literacy, but this is not always the key concern. However, such issues tend not to be raised directly with the learners or their parents.

There is some evidence that this strategy is effective, not only from the case studies, but also from the research literature on the topic. Fraser and Ross (2004) commenting specifically on the Scottish Executive initiative, point to the demand for small grants from the Executive's resources allocated to the literacy strategy. They also point to the responses of parents and carers, using terms such as 'delighted' and 'surprised' at the success of the scheme. Bird (2005) draws attention to 'the influential role of parents in developing children's language and early reading skills' as well as to the need for programmes to be supported by professional development. She also points out that there is also a 'need for more research into basic issues: for example, there is no clear evidence that combined family literacy programmes are more beneficial than separate programmes for adults and children' – this referring to instances where basic literacy may be a concern for parents as well as their offspring. Nonetheless, the evidence, both from the 2005 case studies and from the literature, seems to suggest that these story bag strategies are in themselves effective – which would be suggested by their widespread adoption by classroom professionals. However, like other such initiatives, it will be most interesting to observe whether or not they continue once the initial spurt of interest has passed and – crucially – if the funding to sustain them is withdrawn. There are also some concerns of staff development, for instance, in initial teacher education and in the development in staff of particular skills related to working with parents in the community.

The strategy has also been adopted more widely in the UK – for instance, Reading is Fundamental, a project of the National Literacy Trust, promotes the use of story bags as only one of a large number of strategies to address general literacy concerns (RIF, 2006). The process of working with the book resource would appear to have larger benefits than literacy alone: for example, the parental bond and sense of family purpose would appear from the comments of parents in the case study schools to have been strengthened. It would appear to have a much wider applicability than solely as a strategy specifically targeted at the raising of attainment in boys. While there is merit in this outcome, this is an example where gender is included as part of a set of wider strategies to raise attainment but, as we argued earlier, one of the concerns is that the specific issues raised by gendered patterns in literacy where there are groups of boys who are failing may be overlooked.

Primary years' strategies to improve literacy

Clearly, early years' strategies have considerable influence and applicability in primary schools. In the case study schools, a variety of practice was observed and commented upon, including some strategies which were specifically designed to support fathers working with their sons. There were also instances of early years' story sacks in use more widely in some primary schools, and there was one instance observed of primary schools working together to implement a common literacy strategy. Some primary schools had participated in the bags of books strategy for a limited time, due to the local authority funding a specific initiative related to the national literacy strategy, and it was interesting to note that these schools expressed a desire to continue with the innovation.

One authority has a programme entitled Blokes and Books. This is a part of an early intervention approach aimed at schools which the authority considered would benefit from support in raising attainment in reading. Profiles were constructed using schools' own data on 5–14 attainment, tests on entry and year-end tests and deprivation indices in order to determine those schools most likely to benefit from focused intervention. The Blokes and Books strategy is aimed at promoting parental involvement in supporting children's reading. There is a training session for fathers and a gift of a book token to buy the child's favourite book. Thereafter, there are considerable similarities with the story sacks technique, but the difference is that this initiative is specifically targeted at fathers reading with their sons. The school which was a case study for the 2005 research was one of those identified by the authority as requiring support in this area. Interestingly, though, the school itself did not consider gendered attainment to be a particularly significant issue: in fact, one parent reported that his daughter was the only girl among 11 boys in the class's top group. The strategy was aimed at the middle years – at the P5 level. Two teachers were engaged in the initiative, and there had been some staff development. The authority has engaged the services of consultants, one of whom is a noted expert in the area of reading and children's literacy. The major strength of this particular initiative is that it encourages youngsters to continue to read, after the initial impetus of the early primary years. However, in common with comments made in a large number of the case study schools, staff regretted that they were unable to reach the fathers of those children whom they considered to be most at risk. There are various reasons which can be put forward for this lack of success in engaging with fathers, including a perception that it is mothers who are involved, lack of confidence and this remains a significant issue in gender policy and education. There were also some caveats about the sustainability of the programme. Nevertheless, the school community – children, parents and teachers – felt that the strategy was effective, and that reading was seen as a fun and fulfilling activity for all involved. In this strategy as with others the focus is on the general principle of promoting effective learning which is, of course, vital. However, some of the barriers, such as the lack of involvement of fathers, remain.

In two closely related primary schools, also in a rural context, there was a very interesting initiative involving Getting the Best out of Boys (Condie *et al.*, 2005, pp. 32 ff.). The location in question is one which has suffered from chronic structural unemployment and social deprivation following upon the collapse of local industry, and consequent family dislocation and upset to traditional gendered social patterns. These schools also worked with broader gender-related social participation initiatives and indeed tried to address the particular issue of the involvement of fathers in their children's education. One such, Men and Their Children or MATCH, was locally funded by the authority and engaged fathers in playing and learning with their children in activities held on a Saturday. Where there were many changing and sometimes dysfunctional family units, staff reported that they felt these activities were useful in strengthening family bonds as well as in raising standards of learning. Other strategies also in place were seen as useful in enhancing the relationship between parents and children. One such strategy was Children and their Parents Enjoy Reading (CAPER), which involved the story bags that have been described above. Again, local authority funding was in place in order to support these initiatives. In both primary schools – associated with the same secondary school, with which they worked very closely – there was a clear perception that the changes in the nature of the family had involved a lack of suitable male role models and embedded gender stereotypes which were felt to be generally unhelpful to the advancement of learning.

The CAPER initiative had ensued from a joint staff development session held with colleagues from the secondary school. In the primary schools, staff had continued to attend conferences and were very aware of research, for instance, that of Prashnig on learning styles (Prashnig, 1998). Much of the strategy was based upon the importance of the schools' perceptions of learning styles. Boys, they felt, preferred more active learning styles, although there was a notable lack of dogmatism about this: the schools preferred to concentrate on the individual pupil and what the learning preferences of that pupil were. Pupils and parents (in general) clearly valued the schools very highly and were committed to what was happening. One of the notable features of this particular strategy was that there was in each of the two primary schools a clear sense of leadership from the top, and an equally clear sense of the vision being shared by the staff. Tackling literacy issues amongst boys was a priority because of the gendered patterns of attainment in this area, and it was felt that the multi-layered strategy involving learning styles, choice and engagement in reading, high degrees of parental involvement, support and funding from the local authority and an attempt to grapple with the social difficulties which were besetting the area were showing evidence of success. Interviews with parents would also suggest that this was the case.

The case studies outlined here raise a number of questions in terms of policy and practice in relation to gender. Firstly, the case study above has a number of different strands and is reliant on funding and direction for school leadership and illustrates the importance of there being an understanding by both practitioners and policy makers of the complexities of gender and the intersection of gender and other factors, in this instance economic and social disadvantage, which can militate against success in learning. Secondly, there is the lack of direct engagement of parents in discussions about gender and education and perhaps this might be seen as a lost opportunity. However, finally there is this tension between creating strategies to engage all learners in high quality learning experiences and the need to focus specifically on issues related to the learning needs of specific groups of boys and groups of girls. How far these strategies can be viewed as effecting profound change in attitudes and expectations in relation to boys' attainment in literacy is a matter of debate, as often the means of evaluating this is informal and relies predominantly on perceptions of those involved. That such experiences are regarded as 'fun' is vital, but we also need to adopt a critical stance in looking at the impact of such strategies in relation to gender equality.

The creation of a 'literacy space' for families between home and school is discussed by Pahl and Kelly (2005). The MATCH activities would appear to fit into the category which they advocate, namely one which is not driven by the demands of the school curriculum and which therefore prioritises the needs of formal learning, but rather one where adults and their children can come together on equal terms. Likewise Cook (2005) endorses the 'third space' theory as representing an effective means of bringing communities together for learning and literacy. Torsi (2005) comments briefly on the role of fathers as role models in the literacy process and refers to the National Reading Campaign's Reading Champions scheme. The literature, in fact, suggests that within the parameters of the available research – and depending on the view which is taken of the importance of role modelling – these two primary schools are evidence of very best practice in this area. The results of the research done for the 2005 SEED study would certainly indicate this, too. A further school in this authority was also investigated, and like the two schools mentioned, was also engaged in the CAPER initiative. Reading scores for boys in this school, as well as in the two collaborating primary schools, had risen over the time when the strategy had been in place, although attainments by boys remained lower than those of girls. Like the other schools, this school had perceived a need to raise reading attainment in boys as a priority, although, it, too, accepted the importance of dealing with all pupils' individual needs.

Discussion

At the point where Curriculum for Excellence (SEED, 2004), the policy to revise and develop the curriculum to meet the needs of the twenty-first century in Scotland, is about to become more than a glimmer in the eyes of the Scottish Executive and where it will be a reality in the classrooms of the future, it is interesting to note that those charged with the planning of it have engaged in reviewing the research literature on language and literacy during the process of curriculum design and formation (Smith and Ellis, 2005). This is perhaps in marked contrast to the situation in the design of the previous 5–14 English Language curriculum, where design was influenced by key thinkers in the policy community rather than by research perspectives (McPhee, 1996). It is also interesting to note that schools are already working within the key areas of social and cultural understandings, towards the concepts of responsible citizenship and successful learning identified in the *Framework for the Curriculum for Excellence* (2004). The embedding of literacy and numeracy as key skills in that framework indicates continuity with previous curricular frameworks dating back many years, but the concept of these skills within an entitlement for effective and successful citizenship is perhaps rather different. It will be interesting to see how this particular framework, with its extended remit from 3 to 18, evolves in practice and whether or not it will strengthen the kind of practice which was observed in the 2005 SEED gender study, particularly in the primary schools to which reference has been made above, and whether this practice will be extended to other schools and areas. Ultimately, if the Curriculum for Excellence within the National Priorities takes full effect, literacy will be the entitlement of all, boys and girls alike.

CHAPTER 4

ORGANISING BOYS AND GIRLS: ARE SINGLE-GENDER CONTEXTS THE WAY FORWARD?

Jean Kane

Introduction

The question of class management and how learning is organised is well recognised as an important aspect in gender and education. This chapter considers class organisation and, in particular, the practice of single-gender groupings as a strategy in raising attainment and in improving girls' and boys' whole experience of schooling. Gender as the main organiser of teaching groups is considered here but gender is a factor in other groupings, for example, ability groupings where gendered patterns are a secondary effect, with high- and low-ability groups having a preponderance of girls and boys respectively. Single-gender classes have been used by some schools as a means of addressing gender inequalities, particularly in attainment and we explore a case study of the use of single-gender classes in three secondary schools where such practice had been notified to the local authority as part of schools' endeavours to raise attainment. The case study is further discussed below but, first, a broader context is set for that discussion. Studies of gender in school settings are considered with a view to locating a rationale in the literature for gender-specific groups. Then studies of gender as a factor in class organisation are considered before an account is given of practices in three secondary schools in this particular study. Finally, the chapter provides comment on the effectiveness of this strategy.

Rationale for single-sex groupings

Riddell (2000), in tracing the history of gender in education policy in Scotland, notes that both national advice and local authority policy, although identifying gender factors in, for example, patterns of subject uptake, did not problematise these findings in relation to school practices. That was instead left to teachers' organisations, notably the Educational Institute of

Scotland (EIS) and the General Teaching Council (GTC). In a pamphlet to its members intended as 'a positive assertion against sexism' the EIS criticised the situation in classrooms of the time where:

- Boys demand and receive a generous share of teacher time.
- Boys receive a disproportionate share of hands-on experience (e.g. in science or computing).
- Boys receive apologies from teachers when asked to undertake non-traditional tasks.
- Boys are rewarded for being assertive.
- Boys are advised not to act like girls.
- Boys receive a disproportionate share of coveted class materials.

(EIS, 1989: para 3.2.5, page 5: cited in Riddell, 2000)

The EIS pamphlet was founded upon a range of studies throughout the 1980s charting the gendered nature of pupils' experience of school. Boys' dominant behaviour was observed in both primary and secondary education (French and French, 1984; Swann and Graddol, 1988; Bousted, 1988). Often as a control strategy, boys were more likely to be selected by the teacher to respond within teacher-led discussion but boys would more frequently interrupt or initiate a contribution. A significant proportion of the interactions between boys and teachers were negative comments or reprimands. On the other hand, girls were noted as often seeking support from the teacher on a one-to-one basis by asking questions for which they received an individual response (Good *et al.*, 1980; Dart and Clarke, 1988 quoted by Howe, 1997). The gender of the teacher did not emerge as a significant factor in the differential levels of participation by male and female pupils (Whyte, 1984). However, some commentators noted intra-gender differences, noting that it was not all boys who dominated interactions; rather, a small sub-group of boys in each class was the main focus of attention (French and French, 1984).

Since the 1980s, an extensive range of studies internationally on gender have provided insights into gendered patterns of classroom interaction (Howe, 1997; Francis, 2000); and more highly developed understandings of how boys and girls in school settings are actively involved in negotiating their gender, and other, identities (Skelton, 1996, 1997; Francis and Skelton, 2001). In recent research reminiscent of the message conveyed by the EIS in 1989, Francis (2005, pp. 12–13) records girls' experience in classrooms:

The tendencies for girls to seat themselves on the peripheries of the classroom compounds the impression of girls as pushed to the margins of mixed-sex school life. Boys' physical domination of the classroom and playground space has been well documented. In the classroom, boys simply tend to take up more space than do girls. Even when sitting at desks boys tend to sprawl more and take up more room, and when moving around the classroom their activities are more invasive of space.

For almost three decades then, there have been concerns about girls as marginalised within mixed-gender classroom settings. This has been linked to girls' participation in schooling. McLaughlin (2005, p. 54), exploring the psychosocial experience of 'problem' girls, reported that adolescent girls seemed to experience a 'loss of voice' at that stage, losing the 'ordinary courage' to speak their minds. This 'loss of voice' is linked to the social construction of gender (McLaughlin, 2005). Other writers (Osler and Vincent, 2003), too, have commented upon the link between girls' relationships, agency and experience of school. For example, Osler *et al.* (2002) explained the disproportionate exclusion of boys by noting that girls' exclusion from school was much more likely to be self-exclusion in the form of truancy or other disengagement from school and classroom processes.

Just as for boys, though, commentators have noted that there are important differences amongst girls, with particular regard to ability and to which pupils are in a salient position in the classroom (Morgan and Dunn, 1988). Myhill (2002) argues that, in looking at gender and underachievement, it is important to take account of variables other than gender alone. She found that pupils' levels of achievement were a main distinguishing factor in pupils' engagement with whole-class teaching with underachievers, boys and girls, demonstrating reluctant participation throughout schooling. High-achieving girls engaged consistently whereas it was noted that: 'the high-achieving boy is the least consistent, evolving form a position of high participation and involvement in Years 1, 4 and 5 to being the most unresponsive of all four [groups] in Year 8' (Myhill, 2002, p. 345).

Duffield (2000) found that girls' ability or attainment would also impact on participation levels and the provision of individual support. Social class was noted as shaping gender statistics on attainment. Plummer (2000) argues that some, mainly middle-class, girls are doing well but that other, working-class girls are faring badly in school systems. There are also indications that girls may be penalised for taking a more active role, with evidence of a tendency towards the negative characterisation of girls' assertive and more public behaviour (Reay, 2001; Skelton, 2002). Francis (2005, p. 14) illustrates how both girls and boys cooperate to construct genders as opposite. This negotiation process encompasses the negotiation of a number of femininities, but Francis (2005) and Reay (2001, p. 164) note that although there are multiple femininities, what they all have in common is their deferment of power to the boys: 'Within both localised and dominant discourses that these children draw on being a boy is still seen as best by all the boys and a significant number of girls.'

Sukhnandan *et al.* (2000) noted girls as being, in general, well disposed to the demands of classroom activity. They placed a high value on the presentation of their work; they spent more time trying to improve what they produced (MacDonald *et al.*, 1999); they cared more about the opinions of their teachers (Davies and Brember, 1995; Bray *et al.*, 1997); they derived more enjoyment from school life (Arnot *et al.*, 1998); and all of these factors were in contrast to boys' general attitudes.

This brings us to the second main theme underpinning attempts to address gender inequalities through class organisation. If girls were noted as dominated and marginalised in mixed-gender settings, those same settings were thought by some also to limit boys' attainment. The 'underachievement' of boys was attributed in part to the use of pedagogies unsuitable to boys' preferred learning styles and to curriculum content inappropriate to boys' interests. Even more influential than those explanations of boys' lower relative performance in public assessment systems has been the notion of boys' peer groups and the pull exerted on boys away from school values and norms (Barber 1994; Jackson, 2002). Where the culture of the peer group is to devalue schoolwork, it is difficult for individual boys to seek and accept the public endorsement of the school. Girls, on the other hand, do not experience a conflict of loyalties between friends and school to the same degree (Barber, 1994; Macrae and Maguire, 2000). Studies conducted in English schools recently have tried to research gender in terms of the contradictions and tensions beneath the surface of stable, settled and coherent masculinities (Reay, 2002; Skelton, 2002; Francis, 2005). Renold (2004, p. 373) set out to explore how boys live out various contradictory and hierarchical layers of masculinity and to understand 'the processes by which some boys manage, negotiate (and seek to resolve) the tensions between the perceived feminisation of academic success/studiousness and the pressures of hegemonic masculinity'.

For schools, these two themes in gendered experience – girls' participation and boys' negotiations of particular masculinities – have pointed towards a number of approaches to address inequalities in attainment, including the use of gender as a basis for class organisation. Some of these initiatives have been the subject of systematic investigation. Those studies are considered in the next section.

Main studies and their findings

Three classroom organisational strategies have been developed to tackle gender differences in achievement: the use of particular strategies within mixed-gender groupings; single-gender groupings and classes; and gender-specific groupings to address particular curricular areas or topics. This section discusses findings from the literature in relation to these three forms of class organisation.

Mixed-gender groups

There is little consistent analysis of the use of particular strategies within mixed-gender classes in the literature; this is dealt with largely in material intended for practitioners. Noble and Bradford (2000) argue for a policy on seating in the classroom to prevent pupils, predominantly disengaged boys, gathering at the periphery of classrooms. A common theme in the advice is the use of other pupils to provide advice, to act as role models and to work with pupils who may be disruptive or less engaged. Frequently, these strategies are advocated on the basis of mixing genders. There is a need to be cautious about the implications of some of these proposals which are based upon gender stereotyping. For example, among the suggestions generated by Noble and Bradford (2000) to improve boys' performance are that 'the lads' should be seated next to well-motivated girls who would sort them out and set a good example and, further, that it might be possible to get their girlfriends to make them see sense. Although it must be noted that, in this case, these are among a list of suggestions generated by pupils, the use of girls in the control of boys is something that is implicit in a range of strategies such as seating policies, mixed-gender pairs and groups. Critics are sharp in their responses to advice that girls be used to exercise their 'civilising' influence in 'supporting' boys' learning (Raphael Reed, 1999) and 'to police, teach, control and civilise boys' (Epstein, 1998, p. 9). The expectation that at least some girls should play this role raises questions about the prioritising of some pupils' (boys') learning over others' (girls') learning.

Single-gender groups and classes

The use of single-gender groups has been well-established as an equal opportunities strategy to promote girls' participation and active engagement in areas where girls were under represented such as science, technology and computing (Reay, 1990). The purpose behind the use of single-gender groups was to create a space for girls (Kenway *et al.*, 1998) to actively engage in practical tasks rather than either be passive observers or take on roles such as organising and tidying up. The current use of single-gender classes is largely a strategy used in secondary education to tackle boys' 'underachievement'. One view popularly advanced to explain boys 'underachievement' is that during adolescence boys are distracted by the presence of girls (Woodhead, 1996) and engage in behaviours that detract from their learning. By this account, single-gender classes would overcome a significant barrier to boys' achievement – that is, the presence of girls in the classroom. The effectiveness of single-gender classes for this purpose has been difficult to evaluate because the practice has been very recent. Warrington and Younger (2003) found that it was difficult to assess the impact of single-gender teaching because of the diversity of practices and the limited time during which the approach had been implemented.

As to the more general use of single-gender classes, Warrington and Younger's (2001) study focused on a rare, perhaps unique, co-ed comprehensive in England where single-gender classes had been used for decades. This offered an unusual opportunity to study single-gender classes as a well-established approach to class organisation. In this study, it was noted that a number of factors impacted upon the effectiveness of single-gender classes. Other methods of organising classes were used alongside a gender basis, particularly the practice of setting or ability grouping. The effectiveness of single-gender classes varied according to whether they were 'top' or 'bottom' sets, or pupils performing at the borderline, that were thus organised. There were also clear differences in the level of preparation and level of involvement of pupils, parents and teachers. The involvement of pupils in the planning of the strategy varied widely from a limited briefing to more extended consultations including explanations of the positive outcomes expected. In some schools pupil briefings were conducted through single-sex assemblies. Consultation with teachers was similarly varied: in some schools there was very little preparation and discussion amongst staff; in other schools there was detailed consideration of teaching in single-gender contexts. Parents were noted as having least participation in the decision-making related to single-gender classes, with schools usually limiting the involvement of parents to informing them about the development either by letter or through parents' evening. Parental response was limited, with some positive response from parents of Muslim girls.

Some commentators (Warrington and Younger, 2003) have noted that single-gender classes could be adopted to support the learning of both boys and girls, whilst others (Jackson, 1998, p. 44) observed discernible differences between all-girls classes and all-boys classes, noting that 'girls are liberated by girls-only space' and that there was a more relaxed and supportive environment. In contrast, the climate of boys' groups was reported to be more competitive and aggressive. Warrington and Younger's (2003) survey found the following reasons for adopting single-gender teaching as a means of supporting both boys and girls:

- to encourage able girls to become more involved in lessons and to boost confidence in scientific abilities;
- to encourage boys to work more collaboratively and to develop the social skills necessary for working in mixed groups in subsequent years;
- to address the underachievement of boys, and specifically in some schools the gender gap in English and/or modern languages;

- to limit the effect of boys' bad behaviour, to lessen boys' need to be 'laddish'.

A number of schools in this study talked about different teaching and learning strategies for boys' and girls' groups. Considerably fewer strategies were suggested for girls and these largely revolved around perceptions of girls' strengths or preferences: girls having longer, more in-depth tasks, more reading and writing and increased co-operative activities. Warrington and Younger (2003) reported that it was only on some occasions that the use of single-gender classes was taken as an opportunity to vary teaching and learning approaches. On those occasions, boys' lessons were more structured, they had more variety of activity, more teacher-driven momentum, and less need for sustained attention. Sukhnandan *et al.* (2000) suggested that single-gender classes could benefit boys, not only because of the teaching strategies used, but also because they enable boys' stereotypes to be challenged. In some schools there were modifications to curriculum materials to accommodate perceived differences in interest between boys and girls. This was not a common feature of single-gender classes. Warrington and Younger (2001) reported no differences in curriculum content in a school with long-established single-gender class organisation.

The use of single-gender classes has been reported as being used in Scottish schools. Buie (2004) cites the use of single-gender classes in S2 for English where the boys' performance improved remarkably. Attribution of effect to single-gender classes is difficult here because it was also noted that a teacher with widely acknowledged expertise had been deployed in this classroom. The practice was not continued. Mixed-gender pairings have been used instead, but girls' resentment of this is acknowledged. Positive outcomes in terms of mathematics and language have been noted in another school where there was a longer-term use of single-gender classes (Smith and De Felice, 2001). Elsewhere, early findings in a study of the use of single-gender groups in mathematics were inconclusive (Rowe *et al.*, 1996; Rowe, 1998).

A refinement in the use of single-gender classes has been the matching of teacher gender to pupil gender. It has been noted that these efforts to ensure 'effective' role models by providing male teachers to teach boys and female teachers to teach girls may only serve to consolidate gender stereotypes (Kenway *et al.*, 1998), reinforcing a 'laddish' culture in boys-only classes (Mills, 2001) and further disadvantaging girls within wider school cultures. Francis and Skelton (2001, p. 194) comment: 'many of the "pragmatic" strategies aimed at improving boys' achievement actually compound the construction of gender difference and stereotypes, and sometimes run the risk of marginalising girls'.

However, Warrington and Younger (2003) found no evidence that female and male teachers used different approaches when teaching same-gender or different-gender groups and there is a view that effective single-gender teaching does not rely upon the gender of the teacher.

There is clearly a debate about the impact single-gender classes on pupil attainment. Although the effectiveness of single-gender classes as a means of raising attainment is unclear, some schools reported improved results as a consequence of such strategies. In those schools, the salient factors were:

- Staff were involved.
- Staff were enthusiastic and committed to single-gender teaching.
- Appropriate strategies were planned and implemented in the classroom.
- Teachers shared ideas with other teachers.
- Pupils and parents were involved in the rationale for teaching in single-gender groups.

Some negative effects were detected by Warrington and Younger (2003). Boys' laddish behaviour was noted as having increased and in six schools in this study, the worsening or lack of improvement in boys' behaviour led to single-gender teaching being abandoned. Single-gender classes are, as Warrington and Younger (2003, p. 348) argue, 'no panacea for the problem of poor behaviour, disaffection and lack of achievement'. Nevertheless, as Sukhnandan *et al.* (2000, p. 249) found, 'they can provide a positive and successful experience for girls and boys where the senior management team is committed to single-sex teaching as a mode of organisation through time and to diffuse good practice which might be identified'. However these need to be accompanied by a critical stance and a preparedness to challenge practices that reinforce stereotypical gendered roles.

Subject-specific single-gender classes

There are some examples of single-gender teaching being used as a strategy within particular areas of the curriculum such as personal and social development, sex education and physical education. Strange *et al.* (2003, p. 213) found that the majority of girls and about a third of boys would like sex education in single-gender groups. Some of the reasons put forward by girls include not just the disruption created by boys but 'the subject matter provides boys with an opportunity to use sexual matter and language to denigrate girls'. Sex-based harassment has been cited as a possible reason for single-gender classes, with teachers normalising and accepting sex-based harassment by boys (Kenway *et al.*, 1998). Warrington and Younger (2003) found no evidence of sex-based harassment in their study and no justification for single-gender classes from that source. Staff and pupils in their study construed single-gender classrooms as pleasant and safe places for girls. The findings, however, are not always clear. In a recent survey on sexual health in Scotland, it was found that some children and young people preferred single-gender classes while others felt they learned more from mixed classes, especially on relationship issues (Children in Scotland, 2003). There is a further issue in relation to sex education and children from ethnic minority backgrounds. In some schools in Edinburgh, it was noted that pupils, particularly girls from ethnic minority backgrounds, were being withdrawn from sex education classes. In the consultation conducted by Edinburgh University (Children in Scotland 2003) it was found among those parents who supported sex education that the preference was for single-gender classes.

In a case study conducted by Airnes (2001) on the use of single-gender classes in biology, boys and girls reported very differently on the experience. Whereas boys reported there was no difference in working in single-gender classes, the girls reported that they found this a better working environment. Airnes concluded that there may be benefits in using single-gender groups flexibly and for *ad hoc* purposes, for instance, for practical work or to cover sensitive topics in the syllabus.

Scottish study: findings

In Scotland, the survey (Condie *et al.*, 2005) of strategies to address gender inequality identified three secondary schools where single-gender classes were in use. The schools were in the same local authority but served very different catchment areas. It is important to note that single-gender classes were used in a limited way in each of the case study schools and also that this particular strategy had been used for a short period of time. There were strong similarities in the purposes behind single-gender classes in these schools and in the methods of implementing this strategy. These similarities, and some differences, in the experiences of the three schools are outlined below along with staff and pupil perspectives on the practice.

In all three cases, the strategy was used in a limited way, usually in S3 and S4, although one school had extended the use of single-gender classes into S2. The practice of gender-specific groups in these schools was tied up with other strategies to raise attainment, particularly with ability setting in S3 and S4. Setting by ability was noted as causing a gender imbalance in groups. In one school in particular the 'top' set had been largely girls and the 'bottom' set largely boys. Prior to the use of single-gender classes, there had been 22 girls in the top set and 4 boys whilst the bottom set had 15 boys and 2 girls. There were issues, therefore, in some pupils being in a significant gender minority in some classes. Gender-specific groups were perceived as a way of addressing concerns about gender minorities.

The middle stages of secondary school were cited by staff as the ideal time to change from mixed-gender to single-gender groups. Fourteen- and fifteen-year old boys and girls were seen as benefiting socially and educationally from the experience. Boys' and girls' consciousness of the other gender was heightened at that age and some staff detected a tendency for boys and girls to 'show off' in mixed-gender groups.

Also limited was the range of subjects in which single-gender strategies were used. In the schools in this study this organisational strategy was used either in English and mathematics or in English alone. The focus on these subject areas in S3 and S4, and the intention to tackle middle bands of attainment was directly related to the drive to attain improved Standard Grade outcomes for individual pupils and in schools' overall performance. The initiative was linked to wider school development processes and coordinated by senior management in only one of the three schools. In that school formal monitoring and evaluation took place and these activities were related to the measurement of attainment. Although the raising attainment motive was the main reason shaping the implementation of single-gender classes, other qualitative gains were anticipated in some cases. For example, one English teacher indicated that girls- and boys-only classes in that subject allowed more space for girls and boys to raise and discuss issues related to emotions in ways that would not have been possible in mixed-gender settings.

The remit of the study discussed here related to gender and inequities in attainment but the literature, and participants in the study, recognised that gender is also an important variable in other school processes and outcomes, for example, in behaviour referrals and exclusions. Boys' relative disengagement and disaffection from schooling has been attributed in the literature to the influence of masculine peer groups and to boys' construction of academic pursuit as 'feminine' (Jackson, 2002). Gender-specific classes were identified by some professional participants as addressing wider gendered patterns in schooling. Single-sex classes were noted as a means of counteracting the negative power of the peer group and allowing pupils greater scope to do well at school. Bottom sets emerged as a problem for some teachers in this study, with some noting that low-attaining single-gender groups of boys were difficult to manage, especially when they were larger. In such cases, it was reported, there was a constant need to focus on behaviour. A great deal of teacher time was taken up with this and the pace of the course was consequently slower.

Across the three schools, single-gender classes were instituted as a means of addressing pupil attainment, although secondary purposes related to the classroom behaviour of girls and boys were also cited as reasons for this form of class organisation. Raising attainment was cited as the reason for single-gender classes in all three schools, but the exact nature of the relationship between raising attainment and single-gender classes was not clearly articulated in interviews. One school conveyed their understanding that boys needed different kinds of learning experiences from girls. Boys were reported as needing 'a quick start' to lessons, more structure within lessons and tasks with small, sequential steps as opposed to more open learning tasks. In the same school, girls, too, were cited as potential beneficiaries of single-gender classes which were perceived to offer opportunities to build girls' confidence and self-esteem and to allow them scope for greater participation in lessons. A further purpose linking increased attainment to gender-specific groups was that this strategy enabled curriculum content to be customised for boys, thus increasing their engagement with the curriculum.

The case for single-gender classes was not made whole-heartedly in any of the three schools. Teachers were able to cite reasons why the strategy *might* work, but there was little evidence as yet that it had a significant impact on attainment. The purpose of gender-specific groups related to raising attainment. In two schools, it was noted that there had been no discernible impact on attainment. In the third school, attainment was thought to have improved to some degree in some classes. Even there, though, it is difficult to make a direct link between raising attainment and single-gender classes because ability setting also pertained. Evidence as to the broader impact of single-gender classes on pupils' and teachers' whole classroom experience was also conflicting. Some teachers thought it more enjoyable to work with single-gender classes, finding it easier to build rapport with pupils. Other teachers were less convinced, citing increased behaviour management problems with single-gender classes. Pupils also conveyed mixed views. Girls talked about being able to give their opinions and not be embarrassed in girls-only classes, reflecting boys' and girls' concerns about mixed-gender groups where they had to worry about 'what others would be thinking or saying about you if you answered'. Girls' and boys' responses to the social impact of single-gender groups were also mixed. Some girls expressed relief at the removal of badly-behaved boys from their class but other girls said that some of their friends were boys and they missed them in class. There was agreement that relationships with teachers and attempts to make lessons interesting were more important than gender-based groups. Pupils shared a view that a good teacher was 'someone who made you work but also had a laugh with you'.

Overall, it was difficult in this study to assess the impact of single-gender classes on attainment, or on wider pupil experience. The strategy had been in use only in the short-term. It had been coupled with ability setting and this made the issue more complex. The next section will discuss this complexity and other issues arising from the study.

Gender-specific approaches?

As with other school change strategies with and without a gender dimension, effective implementation required purposeful and collaborative approaches to change, and commitment over a period of time. Gender-specific classes had been in use in all three schools for too short a time to allow proper evaluation of the effectiveness of this strategy. Indeed, this has been a problem more generally with reports from similar initiatives in England also noting difficulty in drawing clear conclusions about the value of these approaches because of the timescale involved and because of other variables impacting on outcomes. In all three schools, the aim of gender-specific classes was to raise attainment but there was less agreement as to how this would actually happen. Sometimes, professional participants communicated a sense that a change in the culture of classes would allow greater participation. This seemed to be true where the culture had been 'feminised' in all-girl sections but a corollary of this was also true – that all-boy classes had enhanced anti-school cultures. A further link between raising attainment and gender-specific classes might have been that they enabled changes in pedagogy and even in curriculum content to accommodate gendered patterns of learning. There was no evidence of this in this study that learning and teaching approaches had been systematically reviewed and developed in the light of the decision to establish single-gender classes. In any event, such approaches would have been contentious, relying as they do upon a highly dichotomised view of girls' and boys' learning and ignoring important intra-gender differences (Skelton, 2002). With regard to the effectiveness of single-gender approaches, Warrington and Younger (2003, p. 351) concluded:

> Single-sex teaching has the potential to raise achievement levels in some contexts, but that this potential will only be maximised when differential teaching approaches are systematically planned and explicitly implemented, monitored and evaluated.

As previously discussed, gender theorists have noted the existence of a range of femininities and masculinities, and that these are all negotiated within school settings and elsewhere (Connell, 1995, 2002; Reay, 2002; Skelton, 2002). Some of these femininities and masculinities are difficult to inhabit, attracting unwelcome attention from peers and staff in schools. Other masculinities, in particular, are powerful and high status within the peer group but may be very challenging for schools. Where gender is used as a basis of class organisation, it would be important that there is no endorsement of a single or 'laddish' version of masculinity, nor communication of a passive and powerless stereotype of femininity. Schools' constructions of masculinity and femininity would also have to be fluid and capable of change. For example, there are indications that femininities are changing. Recently, in a front-page lead story, *The Herald* (18 September 2006) reported that the number of girls involved in crime in Scotland has increased by 40% in five years:

> More than 4,200 female offenders were referred to Scotland's children's hearing system in 2005–6, new figures revealed yesterday. That is up from fewer than 3,000 in 2000–1, as increasing numbers of girls became sucked into a culture of fighting, drinking and thieving.

There were indications that girls' offences were becoming more serious. This has been attributed to the development of a 'ladette' culture amongst girls with a representative of the Chairs of Scotland's children's panels commenting in the same article:

> Over the years we have moved away from young women coming before us for typical shoplifting offences such as stealing make-up out of Boots. We have moved to a much more serious type of laddish culture. With more assaults and fights over boyfriends, the difference between masculinity and femininity is starting to disappear.

Similarly, most recent statistics on school exclusions in Scotland (Scottish Executive, 2007a) show a tenfold increase in the number of girls excluded from primary schools in the 2005/06 session. The number is still a small proportion of the total number of pupils excluded, but there are indications that girls' behaviour is changing. This is not to concur with the quotation above in saying that girls are becoming more masculine, but there are signs that the range of femininities may be changing. For schools seeking to implement single-gender classes, this requires approaches highly sensitive to the range and changing nature of gendered identities, recognising that there are power relations within each gender group.

Gender groups and ability groups

Of the range of factors shaping the effects of gender-specific classes, pupil ability was to the fore. Empirical studies of the negotiation of pupil identities within school settings encompassed the – for schools – central construct of ability (Reay and Wiliam, 1999; Hamilton, 2002, 2006). Pupil identities were tied up with schooling. Schools as well as pupils were actively involved in the negotiation of pupil identities, mainly through the attribution and withholding of ability labels. Schools impacted upon pupil identities because pupils were seen to internalise school and teacher criteria (Broadfoot, 1996) – pupils took to themselves the school's evaluation of them. Thus, assessment and allocation to particular ability sets impacted upon pupils' sense of themselves.

In this study, single-gender classes were usually also organised into ability sets and that aspect of pupil identity – being seen as 'more able' or 'less able' – intersected with gender and created sometimes very unwelcome effects. Some challenging behaviour was seen to arise from pupils' attempts to resist schools' labelling of them as 'less able'. A 'learning difficulties' label was particularly unwelcome and, in preference, boys would create a 'challenging behaviour' label for themselves. This was particularly clear with bottom sets where the combination of 'bad boy' masculinities and low ability labels created classes which were very difficult to manage. The combined practice of setting by ability and separating by gender could be interpreted as exclusive of some boys, that is, as a way of marginalising pupils who are judged to contribute little to school attainment outcomes and who, through their disruptive behaviour, may even detract from the performance of other pupils and from the school's overall standing.

Conclusion

This chapter asked in its title if singe-gender contexts were the way forward in organising boys' and girls' learning. The answer is that such settings can offer something worthwhile for girls and boys, providing a number of conditions are respected. As is argued both in the Scottish study (Condie *et al.*, 2005) and by Warrington and Younger (2001, 2003) in their studies of the use of single-gender classes in English secondary schools all those affected, pupils, parents and teachers, need to be involved in planning the initiative; to have a shared sense of purpose about its ends and an understanding of the means – the approaches to learning and teaching – through which those ends will be pursued. At present there are a smaller number of instances of the use of this strategy in Scotland and there has been little research focused on the impact of this strategy, but nevertheless schools are considering it as part of their approach to raising attainment. From the case studies in the Scottish research it is noteworthy that the decision to use single-gender groups is often seen largely as just another means of grouping pupils and so is not discussed in any great depth with the pupils or their parents. The actual functioning of single-gender groups requires a great deal of attention because there are both very positive possibilities for both boys and girls but there are some dangers. On the one hand, they offer opportunities for acknowledgement of a range of masculinities and femininities and a forum within which traditional stereotypes of girls and boys might be challenged. On the other hand, there is a real danger that, without proper planning and consideration, single-gender classes will simply reinforce stereotypical gender identities and do so by making other masculinities and femininities more marginalised.

CHAPTER 5

SELF-CONCEPT, SELF- ESTEEM, IDENTITY AND GENDER

George Head

In recent literature regarding gender and identity, there has been a realisa-tion that issues of gender are complex and that oppositional propositions such as boys versus girls are inadequate to help us explain and understand how gendered identities are developed (e.g. Arnot and Mac an Ghaill, 2006). Indeed, in our own and others' research (Rudduck and Urquhart, 2003; Reay, 2006) the main discourse among pupils concerned their identity as learners. Whilst it is not surprising that learner identity is a major dis-course in any educational setting it has to be acknowledged that discourse operates at more than one level. Whilst the explicit discourse may refer to academic learning, there are sub-texts that refer to other influences or spheres of learning that can be referred to as cultural, social and emotional learning, all of which contribute to children's overall development, includ-ing gender identities.

Humes (2006, p. 8) argues that we 'validate our identity and our place in the world' through making sense of our experiences. Rudduck and Urquhart (2003) point out that there are a number of areas and topics of discussion that involve pupils in schools comparing their experiences with those of their peers. Naturally, these include contexts that are specific to school such as academic attainment, changing classes and making compari-sons with other schools. Each of these presents an opportunity for pupils to re-conceptualise their identities as learners and to estimate their own value as learners. Consequently, learner identity tends to be the dominant identity created within schools. Indeed, Rudduck and Urquhart (2003), in their exploration of pupils' perspectives on their own identity at a stage of transition within primary school, could find no evidence of pupils dealing with transition and its surrounding issues and difficulties in any gender-stereotypical ways. Instead, their participants responded to issues of dif-ficulty as learners rather than as either boys or girls. Thus, a simple binary opposition of boys versus girls was inadequate for analysis of children's identity and status from their own perspectives. Similarly, Reay (2006) reports that power relationships among primary school pupils were 'more complicated and contradictory' than traditional binary explanations would suggest. However, as she also points out, learning in schools entails more than academic learning. Haywood and Mac an Ghaill (2006, p. 53) also argue that a singular identity does not adequately allow us to understand and make sense of who we are and our position within a community, and that identity consists of 'a range of subject positions ... constituted by a range of narratives'. They argue that forming identities entails a complex and continuous process to which individuals' multiple social and cultural identities contribute. Within this process of combining, shifting and continually developing multiple identities, 'the cultural philosophical dilemmas involved in conceptualising identity are based upon, first, what gives a thing or person its essential nature and, second, what makes a thing or person the same' (Haywood and Mac an Ghaill, 2006, p. 50).

In schools, therefore, identity, including gender identity, will be understood in terms of local communities and cultures as they are experienced by pupils and their teachers but will likely and understandably be dominated by discourses surrounding learning and associated aspects of school life. Consequently, in Chapters 3 and 4, much of the purpose of the initiatives studied and the subsequent discourse on learner identity focused on attainment. In this chapter, however, I want to pursue an argument that recognises that just as learning in schools is more than academic learning and that schools are places where young people are presented with a wide range of opportunities to create, develop and evaluate their identities as learners (Rudduck and Urquhart, 2003; Reay, 2006), in doing so they are also creating and developing gendered identities that both subvert and reinforce hegemonic masculinities and femininities (Renold, 2004). The next section of this chapter consists of an account of five initiatives that were used as case studies. Some of the arguments developed in Chapter 1 and in Chapter 4 will be reprised here in order to critique salient aspects of these initiatives. The remainder of the chapter discusses emerging issues in a more general sense before offering brief conclusions that argue for a pedagogical approach to addressing gender inequalities but in a more explicit and direct way than has been done in most of the initiatives that were included in the research (Condie *et al.*, 2005).

Working with parents

Of the five initiatives discussed here, two, namely curriculum flexibility and streaming by ability, can be seen as addressing gender indirectly through structural alterations to children's learning experiences. A third, 'Reach for the Stars' addressed gender through rewarding attainment. The remaining two, an early years' initiative involving parents, and another on emotional literacy, could be seen as addressing gender in a more direct way.

One city, with a history of deprivation and relative poverty concentrated in housing schemes and estates, had developed a general inclusion strategy which included initiatives to address parenting skills. Initially aimed at young parents and those living in deprived areas, the parenting initiative had progressively focused on the role of fathers.

The key aims were to develop parenting skills and improve parent–child relationships, with issues of self-esteem and confidence important, particularly regarding men. This programme, the Parents Services Initiative (PSI), was not linked directly to the school system, but operated on Saturday mornings and early evenings and tried to involve parents and pre-school children working on shared activities. It began in one particularly deprived estate and was then extended city-wide. One nursery school within the local authority was visited. In addition to involvement in the PSI, staff had developed a number of small strategies intended to open up choices and experiences to the pupils, particularly boys.

The city also established an Early Years' and Child Care Team (EYCCT) to address aspects of the inclusion agenda and set up the PSI in 2000. The Initiative involved education and social work services as well as the voluntary and private sectors. Two development workers were seconded from their posts in school and social work to support the initiative. They planned, consulted, generated ideas and carried plans through, often running the sessions and workshops themselves. They also took on an advisory role, helping others to develop similar programmes of their own. While schools and nurseries made attempts to involve fathers in events such as induction days, few got involved. This was causing concern. At the same time, a male social work student was placed with the team and he was interested in working with the fathers in ways that would support the development of parent–child relationships.

Through a consultation process, the EYCCT found that fathers did want to be involved, but not through the kinds of groups run for women. They wanted to be more active, more hands-on, and were looking for physical, practical activities. The team started running Saturday morning sessions in neighbourhood centres that would appeal equally to mothers, fathers and their children. Sessions included making books, constructing puppets and kites, storytelling and preparing food, and some were also run in the evenings. They developed a series of parent and child workshops on popular themes such as Monsters Inc., and fathers did turn up with their children. They became much more involved and the team reported that they grew in confidence and their relationships with their children improved. They enjoyed the fact that their children saw them making things and the children were impressed by their fathers' skills. However, they still tended to make comments such as 'See the wife, that's her job' when asked to give a view on children and their schooling.

The workshops were intended to involve fathers in the kinds of activities they could do at home and to give them skills, ideas and suggestions for following up the workshops.

Either parent, or both, could attend any workshop, as they chose, and the workshops attracted a broad range of parents of both genders. In addition, grandmothers frequently attended, and when young mothers came, they often brought someone else such as a parent, partner or friend.

The team took the deliberate decision to demand nothing of parents in terms of commitment to the initiative. Experience indicated that it was difficult to engage some parents in discussing their children and their progress, and many parents did not really want to be more involved than just attending individual workshops. It was also felt that parents would not want to be involved in our focus groups, and attempts to achieve this were unsuccessful.

There are a number of issues that arise from this part of the study. Firstly, there is the relationship between gender and social class. Social class and gender identities are discussed widely in the literature. Particularly relevant here are the arguments that recognise that social class contributes towards identity formation and can also be used as an instrument of social control (Haywood and Mac an Ghaill, 2006; Paechter, 1998). Secondly, there is the related issue of how initiatives can both subvert and reinforce hegemonic masculinity and femininity. As indicated above and in Chapters 1 and 3, social class has a strong influence on gender identity with working-class culture in particular reinforcing traditional, dominant gender identities of the active male and passive female. Although fathers' interaction with their children may well have encouraged them to think about and experience different ways of 'being male', nevertheless to do this within a context of activity sessions, crucially, that were marked out as not 'the kind of groups run for women' could be seen as reinforcing hegemonic masculinity (Paechter, 1998). Renold's (2004) argument that to 'do boy' in non-hegemonic ways can place boys in uncomfortable positions, applies equally to fathers here, and the comment 'See the wife, that's her job' should not be a surprise.

The headteacher in the nursery school was aware of the PSI but described the initiatives that she had taken within the school as being triggered by her observations of the children and how they played and interrelated. She noticed that they tended to play along traditional lines with, for example, girls rarely choosing to play with the construction toys. In role play and dressing up, they tended to conform to stereotypical heroes and role models. She had been further prompted to consider gender differences after she attended a national seminar where the speaker had 'touched on gender', raising issues such as right- and left-side brain dominance. This had made her, and subsequently the rest of the staff in the nursery, more conscious of the criteria used in selecting and buying resources. They avoided buying toys and other resources which could be categorised as 'women's work' – for example, ironing boards – and tried to be 'gender-neutral' in their selections. The headteacher targeted three areas of activity for action: sorting activities; role playing/dressing up; and indoor/outdoor play.

Previously the objects used for sorting had tended to be plastic and of familiar content, (e.g. farm animals, transport). The nursery has introduced a broader range of types of objects (e.g. minibeasts, leaves, artificial flowers), with a greater emphasis on varying colour and texture. Where possible, these were tied into topic work (e.g. the seasons, the jungle). Around St Valentine's Day children were provided with hearts in different materials (e.g. wood, plastic, velvet). Staff also introduced objects such as nuts, bolts and screws to be sorted, compared or sequenced, 'to address the interests of boys'.

According to staff, both boys and girls were happy to dress up using the existing stock of outfits (usually parents' cast-offs), but it was felt that both groups needed greater stimulus for imaginative play. To encourage this, staff introduced new outfits such as magical ones (witch/wizard) in interesting fabrics and, specifically to appeal to the boys, animal print designs and a wider range of character outfits. Both boys and girls appear to have increased their interest in these activities, with boys enjoying dressing up as lions, tigers and the like. While not perhaps as immediately stereotypical as previous costumes, the children tended to use them in gender-specific ways.

Traditionally, pre-5 and some infant classrooms have provided a 'home corner' where pupils can act out the kinds of activities that they see happening in their own homes. It was felt that such activities encouraged stereotypical roles and that other contexts should be provided. At the time of the visit, the nursery had set up a 'Rainforest Hut', with all the facilities that a home corner might have – such as food preparation, seating, tables. In the garden, staff introduced large rubber mats and large toy mice – in addition to the usual outdoor toys – to stimulate active play and the children's imaginations.

In discussing obstacles to further development, the interviewees pointed to a culture barrier between the team and the people they are working to support, as well as a power differential. Although they tried to hand over more of the activity to the parents and involve them more, they felt that there were limits to how much the parents could take on.

There was also concern that, occasionally, such initiatives raised parents' expectations of their future interactions with their children's school, only for them to discover later that the school tried to keep parents out. The team members who were interviewed were of the opinion that this did happen and argued that such schools did not understand that 'if you involve parents early, you make life easier in the long run – if you get them on your side earlier – especially if there are problems'. On the positive side, they noticed how fathers were able to appreciate their own child's abilities and skills – often they were surprised at what they saw their son or daughter do.

For one of the team, the key was the *process* rather than the events themselves. The process was based on consultation, with a lot of time spent planning and listening to the parents and finding out what they wanted. Overall the outcome sought by the team was to set up effective approaches, regardless of whether the parents involved were male or female.

There are plans for further projects, including one that focuses on the role of men as fathers and which will culminate in a photographic exhibition of the fathers they are working with in a range of 'father' contexts. Another idea is to give men the opportunity to network and meet others in similar situations and to share with them the research on the impact of fathers on children's lives, for example, on achievement and delinquency.

The effect of 'boy-friendly' initiatives was discussed in Chapter 4 and it only needs to be reiterated here that they can have the effect of reinforcing as well as challenging hegemonic masculinities:

> While potentially effective in addressing issues of masculinity in schools, these strategies can be counter-productive because they invariably normalize, reinforce and leave unquestioned a narrow and often problematic version of masculinity. (Keddie, 2006, p. 100)

The way in which boys were prepared to dress up and the introduction of nuts, bolts and screws (when one of the observations that acted as a stimulus to the actions was girls *not* playing with construction materials) indicates that whilst there was success in developing some aspects of fathers' relationships with their children, such activities nevertheless may have served, inadvertently, to reinforce the very gendered identities that staff were trying to challenge. This highlights the extremely complex nature of gender identities that can no longer be understood as a simple masculine–feminine, boy–girl binary (Haywood and Mac an Ghaill, 2006; Keddie, 2006; Rudduck and Urquhart, 2003). Staff's understanding of gender as a boy–girl issue, albeit with the insight expressed by one member of staff that the process rather than the events was significant is also significant for the operation of this initiative. This is discussed in greater detail later in this chapter.

Flexible curriculum

Curriculum flexibility can be described as the strategies that schools and local authorities implement when designing a customised curriculum that:

- takes account of their own local circumstances;
- recognises the requirements of their students and communities;
- meets the needs and expectations of all learners;
- meets the demands of stakeholders and society in general;
- encourages increased achievement and commitment to learning.

The school that undertook this initiative was situated in a comparatively affluent area on the edge of a major city, with most of the pupils coming from relatively advantaged homes. In addition, it took pupils from two nearby housing estates, each with some measure of disadvantage. Parents had high expectations, in the main, of their children and the school. The school, in turn, set high standards of behaviour and dress for pupils.

Some 5–6 years previously, an analysis of Scottish Qualifications Authority (SQA) results that raised concern about the underachievement of boys coincided with wider concerns about boys and literacy. At that time various strategies were identified and implemented within the English department to encourage boys to read more, and more widely. From this, a more general strategy for raising attainment was developed. Initially, a limited number of boys-only classes were introduced in a targeted way, that is, with boys who needed more intensive support. However, these were discontinued after 2-4 years and there was, at the time of the research, no desire amongst staff for single-gender classes and very little support from the senior management team for a return to this approach. Other measures taken to deal with underachievement were seen to be meeting the needs of pupils in satisfactory ways, without single-gender classes. Senior staff who were interviewed expressed a clear desire to make sure that any changes were justifiable in educational terms and to take staff and parents along with them in introducing new practices. The local authority was supportive, but had not provided additional funding or staff to support the developments.

In the context of this specific school, curriculum flexibility involved: a modular structure to the curriculum, with shorter targets and blocks of study; class sizes, in the main, at maximum size, allowing greater resource to be allocated to those needing more support; and a timetabling procedure that slotted in the 'smaller' subjects first and fitted the core areas, for example, Mathematics and English, around these, thereby maximising choice.

The school had an inclusion policy, of which gender was an element. Raising attainment, and more specifically, achievement in national qualifications, formed a significant part of the school development plan and were on both the local authority's improvement and operational plans. In these, there was a particular focus on boys' achievement levels, most notably on literacy.

The initiative was originally driven by the depute head with responsibility for learning and teaching and all teachers within the school were involved. The original work in the English department was initiated and driven by the head of department as part of their response to the school development plan. The literacy dimension had diminished in prominence, with the national qualification dimension taking priority.

In 2002–03, the school replaced Standard Grade programmes of work and examinations with National Qualification units for almost all subject areas, and continued to work to achieve this for all pupils and subjects. The pacing of units and assessment events was believed to offer a more coherent learning experience for pupils, encouraging more of them to study for Higher qualifications. In particular, the short timescale of the units was considered more appropriate for boys. Those interviewed agreed that the National Qualification units offered better continuity, coherence, pace and progression than Standard Grade, and had greater relevance to the Higher programmes of study. The school held a number of seminars and staff development events related to the initiative. In addition, there were meetings with parents to share plans and aspirations and gain their support for the developments. The various strands of the initiative were integrated into everyday practice.

The school monitored and evaluated the original initiative and the subsequent developments relating to achievement in national qualifications. The impact received considerable publicity, with the outcomes presented at seminars and reported widely in the press. Copies of slides used in seminars and with parents showed clear educational arguments for the initiatives, including references to research findings. It was stated that there was a belief among staff that gender was not the key factor: that there was a cluster of factors affecting attainment of which gender was only one, albeit a visible and important one. More recently the school has been concerned with the intersection of gender and other factors such as ethnicity and ability.

Staff interviewed thought that a particular strength of the strategy was the fact that it was a whole-school approach that involved parents as well as staff and pupils. Changes had been made to the ways in which they communicated with parents at, for example, parents' nights. Considerable time had been spent on 'awareness-raising' and on consulting with staff, parents and pupils. This had been complemented by in-house staff development on related issues such as learning styles. On the downside, there were some subjects that did not readily adapt to the National Qualifications format. The staff involved in taking the strategy forward had encountered a number of obstacles, including the attitudes of some parents and other staff who had not been convinced of the need for change. In addition, some parents held traditional views of appropriate roles and career options for their sons and daughters.

The first issue that arises in this initiative is what Renold (2004) terms the mythological 'under achieving boy'. She rejects the premise of boys as a homogeneous group that underpins the concept and how that impacts on the measures taken to address their issues. Gender as it is thus constituted has been seen as a matter of attainment and learning styles, and not as gender in its own right. Moreover, the privileging of Maths and English, it can be argued, reinforces a curriculum that resulted from Descartes' separation of mind and body and resulted in a focus on 'mental capacities and dispositions' and a marginalisation of subjects such as PE, sex education and crafts in Western curricula (Paechter, 2006, p. 123). This Cartesian duality mirrors the simplistic masculine–feminine binary that is inadequate for the understanding of gender in education.

Nevertheless, within this initiative there was recognition that pedagogy is a significant factor, that there are a range of influences that contribute to the formation of gender identity and that parents' perceptions are crucial. These issues are dealt with in greater detail later in the chapter.

Developing emotional literacy

One primary school had developed a series of strategies designed to address the very challenging behaviour of some boys: behaviour that was impacting on the attainment of those boys in particular and on the classroom climate generally. The school is a denominational primary school which, in earlier years, had been a combined primary and secondary school. When the secondary department moved to its present location, the primary department remained in the original accommodation and was re-named. Its buildings are traditional and centrally situated. Many parents and grandparents within the community attended the school and maintain close ties with it. The area has suffered from a degree of deprivation in the past.

A strategy had been developed to respond to pupils – mostly boys – in the later stages of primary school who had very challenging behaviour and who seemed unable to manage their own responses to situations. One pupil, in particular, gave cause for concern because of his lack of self-awareness and self-control. The headteacher and the behaviour support teacher (who was also a Primary 7 teacher) believed that there might be benefits in a more direct and sustained attempt to develop emotional literacy in some pupils. Accordingly, parents, pupils and staff were consulted. A high level of support was expressed and the initiative proceeded. No research was identified as contributing to the development. Funding had been made available from the Scottish Executive as part of the national programme, Better Behaviour – Better Learning. This was used to provide cover for the Behaviour Support Coordinator who worked with the extraction group one morning each week.

For one morning a week, the Coordinator worked with a small group of pupils extracted from their ordinary lessons. Activities and tasks aimed, for example, to enable pupils to develop empathy by encouraging them to appreciate the impact of their actions from others' point of view. The approach also aimed to draw parents into thinking more about their children's responses and how these might be developed to improve relationships.

The initiative was relatively small-scale, targeted and *ad hoc* in that it operated in response to the needs of particular pupils, as these emerged. At the time of the visit, the procedure had been suspended for the remainder of the session as it was felt that the need did not exist at that time. It would be revived if a need was identified.

The specific initiative on emotional literacy was linked to other approaches used in the school such as Circle Time. It was perceived that boys had particular difficulties in expressing views and feelings and that the additional support provided in an extraction group for one morning per week would enable them to function more effectively in social situations. It was hoped that their improved behaviour would have positive implications for other pupils in their class and in the school generally.

The approach here was not intended primarily to address boys' under-attainment, nor was it targeted specifically at boys. However, since the extraction group was composed solely of boys, this school's experience reflects a wider situation where there is a significant gender imbalance in discipline referrals and in national exclusion statistics. Concern about boys' performance in school relates to a number of outcomes and not just to attainment. Better Behaviour – Better Learning makes explicit links between learning and behaviour and advocates more integrated systems of pupil support. In that policy context, the work here could be seen to address boys' attainment by supporting their wider development.

Addressing boys' behaviour in this manner, whilst apparently straight-forward, presents teachers and pupils with a convoluted and complex milieu that may in fact result in short-term gains at best and, at worst, a reinforcement of the very behaviour that led to concern in the first place (Head and Jamieson, 2006). Initiatives such as this tend to work on an assumption that 'fixing' behaviour is a prerequisite to dealing with pupils' learning (Head, 2005). Consequently, if gender is generally conceptualised as a matter of attainment (the secondary concern in this case), then these boys are likely to find themselves at a further remove from being able to address their gender issues than their peers. Moreover, by separating them out from their peers, there is a danger that they become seen as 'Other'. Paechter (1998) argues that to some extent all children are 'Other' in school by dint of their power position in relation to teachers and other adults, which is itself male hegemony. She also argues, albeit concerning girls and non-hegemonic boys, that 'differently assigned children are treated differently by... adults' (Paechter, 1998: 43). The boys in this instance, having been assigned to the category of 'difficult behaviour' are likely to be treated as such and have their identity as aggressive, difficult, challenging males reinforced: the very macho, hegemonic masculinity that the initiative was intended to challenge. Similar explanations might apply to the Reach for the Stars (RfS) initiative which we will consider next.

'Reach for the Stars'

The school in which it operated was a denominational secondary, had a mixed catchment area and was situated in a town close to a major city. The school roll was under capacity and accommodation comprised two main buildings with two huts, each containing two classrooms. 'Reach for the Stars' (RfS) had been in operation for 10 years and so was well established within the school. It was originally developed as a response to Promoting Positive Behaviour developments and had a focus on pupils in the first two years of secondary school (S1 and S2). There was a desire amongst staff to shift the focus away from punishment and towards the positive reinforcement of desirable behaviour. The strategy was designed to provide added motivation for all pupils, not just boys.

As with most of these strategies investigated, attainment data had been instrumental in initiating the change in practice. Both the headteacher and the depute head indicated that attainment levels within the school were in line with national trends; girls generally tended to perform better than boys in 5–14 outcomes and in SQA awards.

The initiative involved all teachers, first and second year pupils and their parents and was managed by the coordinator and a team of teacher volunteers whose main role was to organise and run the award ceremonies which formed an integral part of the strategy. Approximately two years ago, the principal teacher (PT) post in developing the ethos of the school was established, providing the coordination for the initiative (the RfS coordinator). In addition, there was a very effective system of distributed leadership wherein teacher volunteers cooperated to implement the various elements (the RfS team). All teachers in the school were involved, although their involvement was not considered to be demanding of their time and the administrative systems were simple and user friendly.

Involvement in the RfS team was regarded as a form of staff development. The key aim of the strategy was to motivate pupils in S1 and S2 by providing a consistent, school-wide system of incentives. All pupils started with a maximum number of 48 points (i.e. four points for each of the twelve subjects on their timetable), but these could be deducted by teachers in any subject. Therefore, the challenge for pupils was to safeguard those 48 points. Points could be regained or awarded in line with four criteria, that is, pupils were required to be caring, prepared, positive and responsible.

In discussions with staff and pupils, two issues arose in relation to these conditions. Some staff felt that they might disadvantage boys by emphasising traditionally 'feminine' qualities such as caring. In the focus group with pupils, there was considerable discussion of these criteria in relation to the consistency of their application. Some teachers, it was reported, gave rewards merely if asked to do so, whereas other teachers required that 'you save somebody's life' before they would allocate rewards.

Award ceremonies were held approximately every six to eight weeks and those who had maintained their tally had their achievement publicly recognised. In addition, teachers could give 'gold awards' and these, too, were recognised at the ceremonies. Approximately two-thirds of pupils would receive an award at each ceremony and a letter would go home to their parents comparing their rating with the year average. The ceremonies were intended to be both educational and fun, and to this end a number of team games and activities were included. (Further details of the RfS project can be found on the National Priorities website (National Priorities, 2007).)

It is readily acknowledged that the strategy is firmly rooted in behaviourist theory and emphasises the importance of rewarding the behaviour the school wants rather than punishing the behaviour it does not want. Yet as argued with the previous initiative, there may be unforeseen negative effects.

The approach here was not intended primarily to address boys' underachievement, nor was it targeted specifically at boys: the strategy was designed to increase motivation to succeed in all pupils. While girls tended to attract more of the rewards, it was felt that the very structured and comprehensive approach to incentives served boys well.

There is ongoing monitoring of the strategy. The coordinator maintains a database in which all returns from teachers are entered. This enables the identification of patterns and trends and the analysis of these by the RfS team.

In the discussion with pupils, behaviour rather than ability emerged as a main distinguishing characteristic of boys and girls. It was also a key concern for the focus group, with one girl advocating that the school should 'put those who do not want to learn in a class of their own'. Girls were thought to worry more about their performance and to try harder. There was agreement between pupils (and some teachers) that boys were more optimistic about their futures. One S2 boy, for example, thought that boys generally believed they could always get an apprenticeship, even if they did not do well in school. Pupils could not comment on whether the strategy had made a difference. It had been operating for ten years and was closely associated with their experience of the school. However, from the focus group discussion with pupils it was clear that the RfS strategy mattered to them. Pupils cared about their performance within it and enjoyed the award ceremonies.

As argued earlier, the understanding of gender identity is more complex than simple binaries. Despite its root in behaviourist theories and its focus on behaviour, there is nevertheless recognition of the importance of social and cultural factors in the formation of identities. There are arguments in the literature that the conceptualisation of boys and girls as separate, homogenous groups oversimplifies our responses to and expectations of the learning and behaviour of young people. Indeed, our own and other studies have shown that powerful girls can behave in similar ways to powerful boys (especially, perhaps, within single-sex contexts) and that 'clever' girls and boys can behave in non-hegemonic ways without exposure to ridicule or embarrassment (see, for example, the instance of the one girl in the 'top group' with eleven boys in Chapter 3).

Streaming by ability

The final case study undertaken by the project team was on the impact of streaming by ability within a secondary school. The school, a denominational secondary community school, was located in a housing scheme on the edge of a city. It is housed in recently built and very attractive accommodation and was one of the first within the city to have its accommodation modernised and upgraded. The new buildings had much improved the school's image within the local community and beyond, and the Head of the Learning Community indicated that he believed there was a strong link between the quality of the physical environment and pupil attainment. At the time of the visit, the school roll sat at about two-thirds of its capacity.

The strategy had been in place for four years. The initial impetus came from the outcomes of an inspection by Her Majesty's Inspectorate (Education) and the development of the follow-up Action Plan, in combination with wider concern and policy development relating to raising attainment. The key aim was to improve attainment levels of all pupils, which were below national standards. The initiative was not supported by any targeted staff development activity.

The strategy centred on the policy of establishing a two-class accelerated stream within the school. It was originally pioneered by the Head of the Learning Community and became embedded in the organisation of the school, and involved all staff and pupils. Sixty pupils in each year were assessed as suitable for inclusion in the scheme on the basis of their 5–14 assessments. These pupils formed two classes of 30, allowing some flexibility to work with smaller groups of the remaining pupils.

Alongside streaming, the school had adopted a number of other strategies for raising attainment. For example, a high priority was given to pastoral care, and two 15-minute sessions were used for mentoring groups of pupils each week. This time was partly devoted to encouraging pupils to think about themselves and their ambitions. Furthermore, the depute headteacher with responsibility for the inclusion agenda coordinated a system called 'Alpha' where more proactive support was given to pupils seen as being vulnerable. In addition, the pastoral care team, augmented by classroom assistants, offered a range of forms of support to certain pupils, including information and computing technology (ICT) programmes and counselling. A number of projects allowed pupils to engage in learning beyond the class-room. The intention was to support pupils to expand their horizons and to consider new possibilities for themselves.

The school used the established systems of local and national data-gath-ering procedures to monitor the impact. These indicated that the school had significantly improved its statistical outcomes for examinations, attendance and exclusions – outcomes that have led to considerable interest from the national press.

Three S5 pupils, all of whom had been in the accelerated stream, took part in a group interview. All three had very clear views of their futures in that they knew that they wanted to continue into higher education and, in two instances, were very clear and well informed as to how they could achieve their aims. For example: 'I am going to do an HND in Social Work and then I would like to do a degree in Child Psychology' (boy, S5). The school reported that parents had accepted the streaming arrangements, even when their child had been placed outside of the accelerated stream. One member of staff believed that this was because they had always managed to convince parents that the school had their child's best interests at heart.

As with the previous initiative, the desire to avoid a 'boys only' or 'girls only' initiative appears effective. Renold (2004) argues in the context of her own study, that it might be easier for white middle-class high achievers to avoid hegemonic genders, but that begs the question of the impact on 'low achievers'. Moreover, the same arguments discussed above about 'clever' boys and girls apply and in this case are compounded by the existence of a category of 'not clever' boys and girls. The danger, therefore, is that, inad-vertently, the identities (including gendered identities) that might want to be challenged may, in at least some instances, be reinforced. This initiative, therefore, represents another example of the complexity of gender issues and the need for educators to understand the nature of gender which we will consider in the final chapter.

CHAPTER 6

TAKING GENDER FORWARD

Rae Condie, Christine Forde and George Head

Tackling gender inequality

This focus of this book has been to place the strategies and approaches adopted by Pre Five and schools to tackle the issue of gender inequality in Scottish schools in a wider context of debates about gender in education. The first issue explored in Chapter 2 was the development of policy on gender and education in Scotland which revealed a huge diversity, with some Local Authorities having explicit policies on gender while others subsumed the issue of gender equality within broader set of policies on inclusive education. As we discussed earlier, there is considerable merit in linking the question of gender to other factors such as social class, race, sexuality and disability which can have a cumulative effect in limiting the opportunities and aspirations of learners within education. However, we also need to concern ourselves with the specific issues that relate to gender, and that in seeking to address these issues we should consider the fundamental question of the ideological construction of gender underpinning polices and practices in education. A concern that arises from the research is the issue of a searching interrogation of the impact of gender (and its intersection with other social factors) in creating barriers to learning and achievement. Policy and many of the practices we examined arise from questions posed by the broad gender patterns evident in national examinations and other attainment data, but such data masks more complex issues in the area of gender and education. The question of literacy is an example of where broad gender differentiated patterns are not explored critically.

There is no doubt about the significance of the development of literacy in overall achievement. Literacy has become a gendered issue within education with the lower attainment of boys in reading and writing, and various projects have been established to encourage boys to read and to support parents, fathers in particular, to read with their sons. These projects have been designed not only to raise attainment but to look at some wider concerns about positive attitudes to learning and the involvement of parents, including in some instances particularly fathers, in their children's learning. These projects have had some very positive outcomes. Nevertheless, questions can be asked about sustaining such projects to ensure the long-term impact on learning and part of the long-term impact is to challenge the ideologies of gender that act as barriers to effective learning and achievement. Therefore we have to consider how far such initiatives challenge expectations based on hegemonic masculinities and femininities which continue to limit opportunities with staff, parents and pupils.

It is perhaps in the discussion in Chapter 4 on classroom strategies that we see most visibly the complexity of the question of gender in education. The introduction of different ways of managing learning such as single-gender teaching has provided more flexible and responsive approaches to supporting the learning of different groups of pupils. However, using gender as a basis for such organisational patterns raises some significant questions. When used flexibly, single-gender classes can indeed have a positive impact but there are significant criticisms, particularly about the reinforcement of those behaviours and attitudes thought to be typical of boys and of girls. Such approaches are often developed as a means of addressing the attainment agenda and there is no substantial interrogation of the assumptions of what it means to be a boy or what it means to be a girl underpinning such strategies. How far single-gender classes and any other organisational strategy teachers use provide opportunities and support for boys and girls to allow expression of other forms of femininity and masculinity is a significant question, for here we are not just dealing with some organisational strategies. Instead, we are dealing with the far more complex question of gendered identities. What is clear from the discussion in Chapter 5 is the profound importance of gender in our understanding of ourselves as individuals and it is to this we now return.

Coming back to the concept of 'gender'

The term 'gender' and what is meant by it emerges as problematic from this research. Paechter (1998) builds on the work of other theorists such as Butler (1990, 1993) and Connell (1995) and sets out an argument for gender as a social and cultural construction and differentiates it from matters of biological sex. The now common distinction between sex (biology) and gender (culture) has led to a focus largely on trying to separate out what differences derive from biology and what differences derive from culture. As Paechter recognises, this is 'an artificial and dualistic distinction' but she argues that it is one that allows her to challenge assumption and expectations posited on a 'direct causal connection' between the two (Paechter, 1998, p. 40). Through this process, she illustrates how gender is constructed socially and culturally in Western society to the extent that: 'As any Western infant teacher will confirm, children in the early years of schooling have tremendously stereotyped views about gender-appropriate group membership and behaviour' (Paechter, 1998, p. 45).

In the range of strategies to tackle gender inequality investigated in Scottish schools (Condie *et al.*, 2005), the social and cultural aspects of the formation of gender identity appear to be overlooked, or in terms of hegemonic gender identities not even realised, in the desire to address gender and other issues as questions of attainment. That this is the case can be illustrated from a focus group with one of the schools involved in addressing literacy. In response to questions regarding what they talked about to each other, primary 5 girls in a school in a predominantly working-class area responded that it was easier for boys as they had football to talk about. These girls were themselves members of a girls' football team but whilst it appeared appropriate for them to play football, discussion of football at home and in school was a predominantly male activity, thereby reinforcing gender stereotypes whilst as the same time seemingly subverting hegemonic femininity. The school, albeit inadvertently, by valorising football may well be reinforcing the gender identities they were otherwise seeking to challenge.

However, the inclusion of fathers in various initiatives and parents generally in matters of achievement opens up opportunities for schools and teachers to address the social and cultural aspects of gender formation. Addressing teachers' and other adults' understandings of gender has been approached obliquely, usually as a matter of attainment or behaviour. Reay (2006, p. 122) argues that schools' 'intense preoccupation with academic success' serves to obscure gender issues. Using gender theories to address issues of attainment and behaviour may well be a more productive approach.

Even a 'gender-first' approach would nevertheless have to avoid a one-dimensional conceptualisation of educational issues. Addressing gender issues as being about boys, boys' underachievement, or boys' behaviour, for example, ignores the fact that to understand oneself as something (in this case, a boy) entails understanding oneself in terms of what one is not (e.g. a girl) (Paechter, 1998). Similarly, Keddie (2006) argues that popular assumptions about active boys and passive girls and the impact these assumptions have on the decisions educators make concerning curriculum and learning styles and activities tend to result in inadequate 'undertheorised and simplistic strategies designed to address issues of masculinity in schools' (Keddie, 2006, p. 100). We need, then, to consider the role of the teacher in the pursuit of gender equality in education.

Developing strategies in the classroom

One of the issues often cited in the popular media is that of the gender of the teacher, particularly when there is an ongoing decline in the number of men in the education professions. However, the gender of the teacher is less relevant than might be popularly assumed. Instead, there is evidence that both boys and girls respond to explicit forms of teaching, curricula and pedagogy that they can relate to and have relevance within their wider experience and to teachers, male or female, who are committed to fostering learning and establishing good relationships with their pupils, both boys and girls (Mills *et al.*, 2007; Carrington *et al.*, 2005). The skill and attitude of the teacher is the critical issue.

Keddie (2006) argues that the teacher is a key influence on what happens in classrooms and argues for a pedagogical approach to addressing gender issues through the productive pedagogies model developed in Queensland. This model provides a framework for a pedagogical process but stops short of discussing how it should be taught. This is often the case with educational initiatives (see, for example, Head, 2005) and just as assumptions are made on undertheorised notions of gender, so the practicalities of pedagogical approaches are often left undertheorised. This may well be fair in that it reflects the boundaries among the functions of academics, policy makers and teachers, and that respecting those boundaries recognises the legitimate territory of others.

The first step in developing a more effective pedagogy to address gender and other issues might be to ensure that teachers are able to engage with theories of gender. Nevertheless, visions of what an appropriate pedagogy for self-understanding and learning might look like are available. Kerdeman (2003) likens the experience to being 'pulled up short'. Kerdeman argues that traditional teaching methods that entail questioning, challenging and instilling doubt have limited effect in comparison with the type of realisation that is experienced in moments of epiphany or revelation (Hogan, 2005). The former entail an assumption that we can choose to challenge our philosophies and beliefs, whilst the latter result when 'our beliefs are thrown into doubt without, and even in despite, prior deliberation on our part' (Kerdeman, 2003, p. 294). Both Kerdeman and Hogan argue that teachers can create the conditions in which these moments are more likely to occur.

Moreover, Osborn (2004) found that there were less gender issues and fewer problems of absence and disaffection within a school in Denmark. This was attributed to the nature of the school involved in which there was an equal emphasis on the affective and cognitive curricula, and in which students had a high degree of control over their learning. However, a combination of personal beliefs, professional approaches and appropriate context may only be most effective when informed by 'a social theory of learning which links the broader socio-cultural setting of the education system with the individual sociocultural biographies and identities of teachers and pupils' (Osborn, 2004, p. 282). Core to these identities would be gender identities.

Where do the pupils fit in?

We come back then to the paradox of gender when we consider the role pupils play. Ideas about what it means to be male or what it means to be female are complex and multidimensional. Strategies based on a limited construction of what it means to be male or what it means to be female may recuperate rather than challenge forms of masculinity and femininity that act as barriers to learning.

Responses to concerns over boys' literacy that promote action stories and male characters, usually in heroic roles, are based on the generalisation that all boys like this kind of literature and reflect a particular view of how boys 'do' boy that ignore the experiences of many young males/boys in our society. They question the extent to which this will improve literacy for all pupils in that it reaffirms a particular model of 'doing' boy. Similarly, Lingard (2003) argues that there is a need to recognise multiple masculinities and to take into account a range of other factors that can disadvantage or disempower particular groups of men.

Kehler and Greig (2005) argue that the hegemonic masculinity that, often implicitly, underpins responses to addressing evidence of boys' underachievement fails to acknowledge the multiple masculinities that exist. Individual males can and do move between and negotiate different masculinities, depending on context and personal circumstances. Their identities are shaped by their race, class, sex and the gender roles deemed acceptable within their social groupings but they also move between different forms of masculinity according to the social context (Kehler and Greig, 2005; Warin, 2006). Thus not only is the 'all boys'/'all girls' distinction a fallacy, so to is the notion that masculinity is a fixed construct for an individual.

One of the issues emerging from this research is the place of pupils in the development of specific strategies to explore and through these initiatives opportunities for the pupils to develop a greater understanding of gender in their own lives, educational careers and long-term aspirations. It might be argued that children in pre-5 and primary education are too young to explore gender, or it is intrusive, or we are not sure of parents' reactions when we are seen to be playing about with gender, mindful of the controversies in the mid 1980s about boys playing with dolls. However, not to engage pupils in what is a critical aspect of their growth as a person as well as a learner is very much a missed opportunity. We have to move beyond a sense that exploring gender with children is simply about getting them involved in non-traditional activities and acquiring attributes usually associated with the other gender. It would appear from the research (Condie *et al.*, 2005) that there are missed opportunities that could afford richer learning experiences if the question of gender was part of the discussion. Instead we have to recognise and promote the pupils' own agency and provide them with understanding of their role in shaping their identity. We often perceive children as passive in the matter of gender upon which we lay expectations. However, we cannot neglect pupils' agency in forming their gendered identity and understandings of gender appropriateness. As Houston (1994) noted, despite teachers' attempts to create a 'gender-neutral' context, pupils not only remain very aware of gender expectations but also have the facility to explore these expectations critically. Helping to develop a critical understanding of the ideological construction of gender can only open up learning opportunities for children and young people.

Moving forward

Within educational policy, we seem locked into an understanding of 'gender' that focuses on the relative positions and success rates of girls and boys, thereby creating a sense that the success of one gender is always at the expense of the other. This is particularly acute when that success is narrowly defined as attainment in national systems of assessment such as national tests or certification. There are two highly significant challenges to this understanding. One is the assumed homogeneity of each of the categories of 'being a boy' and 'being a girl' while the second is the power accorded to gender as a determinant of success in school in the absence of consideration of other influencing factors.

The evidence clearly indicates that gender is only one of a complex interplay of factors that have a bearing on the outcomes of schooling. The broad-brush analysis which attributes advantage or disadvantage to one gender or the other masks the reality that some boys and some girls experience considerable disadvantage while others experience little or none. More effort is needed to determine 'which boys' and 'which girls' and plan strategies accordingly, within a framework for social justice. Strategies that neglect to take cognisance of what counts as social capital for those groups of pupils who experience disadvantage as a result of ethnicity and social class are unlikely to be successful.

Strategies to address gender inequalities should be located within a framework that explicitly acknowledges that there are several factors contributing to disadvantage in schooling and that these can interact and intensify the degree of disadvantage experienced by individual and groups of pupils. They should be based on rigorous research and robust analysis of the data that targets disadvantage and discredits simplistic, stereotypical notions of gender. Such strategies should challenging children and young people intellectually, involve them in reflecting on and challenging stereotypes of all kinds and ask them to consider how they relate to their own experiences outwith school. However, gender *is* a significant factor that influences the outcomes of schooling for many pupils, both boys and girls, but it is complex and simplistic solutions are unlikely to be the answer.

REFERENCES

Airnes, J. (2001) 'Pupils' perceptions of gender segregation in biology', *SCRE Newsletter* No. 69 (online). Available from URL: www.scre.ac.uk/rie/nl69/nl69airnes.html (accessed 30 August 2004)

Alloway, N. and Gilbert, P. (1997) 'Boys and literacy: lessons from Australia', *Gender in Education*, Vol. 9, No. 1, pp. 49–60

Anderson, R. (2003) 'The history of Scottish education', in Bryce, T. and Humes, W. (eds) (2003) *Scottish Education*, Edinburgh: Edinburgh University Press, pp. 219–28

Archer, L. and Yamashita, H. (2003) 'Theorising inner-city masculinities: "race", class, gender and education', *Gender and Education*, Vol. 15, No. 2, pp. 115–32

Arnot, M. (1991) 'Equality and democracy: a decade of struggle over education', *British Journal of Sociology of Education*, Vol. 12, No. 4, pp. 447–66

Arnot, M. (2003) 'Male working-class identities and social justice: a reconsideration of Paul Willis's Learning to Labour in light of contemporary research', in Vincent, C. (ed.) (2003) *Social Justice, Education and Identity*, London: RoutledgeFalmer, pp. 97–119

Arnot M., Gray J., James M., Rudduck J. and Duveen G. (1998) *Recent Research of Gender and Educational Performance (OFSTED Reviews of Research)*, London: The Stationery Office

Arnot, M. and Mac an Ghaill, M. (eds) (2006) *The Routledge Falmer Reader in Gender and Education*, Abingdon: Routledge

Baker Miller, J. (1986) *Toward a New Psychology of Women*, London: Penguin

Barber, M. (1994) *Young People and their Attitudes to School: Interim Report*, Centre for Successful Schools, University of Keele

Barber, M. (2002) 'From good to great: large scale reform in England', paper presented at Futures of Education Conference, Universität Zürich, 23 April

Bird, V. (2005) 'Understanding family literacy', *Literacy Today*, March, p. 12

Black, P., Harrison, C., Lee, C., Marshall, B. and Wiliam, D. (2002) *Working Inside the Black Box: Assessment for Learning in the Classroom*, London: NFER-Nelson

Bousted, M. W. (1989) 'Who talks? The position of girls in mixed sex classrooms', *English in Education*, Vol. 23, No. 3, pp. 41–51

Bray R., Gardner, C. and Parsons, N. (1997) *Can Boys do Better?* Leicester: Secondary Heads Association

Broadfoot, P. (1996) *Education, Assessment and Society*, Buckingham: Open University Press

Buie, E. (2004) 'Fightback by boys reignites debate on single sex classes', *The Herald*, Glasgow, 20 August

Butler, J. (1990) *Gender Trouble: Feminism and the Subversion of Identity*, London: Routledge

Butler, J. (1993) *Bodies That Matter: On the Discursive Limitations of 'Sex'*, New York and London: Routledge

Byrnes, J. P. (2001) *Minds, Brains and Learning*, New York: Guildford Press

Carrington, B. and Skelton, C. (2003) 'Re-thinking "role models": equal opportunities in teacher recruitment in England and Wales', *Journal of Educational Policy*, Vol. 18, No. 3, pp. 253–65

Carrington, B., Tymms, P. and Merrell, C. (2005) 'Role models, school improvement and the "gender gap" – do men bring out the best in boys and women the best in girls?' paper presented to the EARLI 2005 Conference, Nicosia

Children in Scotland (2003) 'Enhancing sexual wellbeing in Scotland: a sexual health and relationships strategy: consultation response from children and young people' (online). Available from URL: www.childreninscotland.org.uk/docs/policy/consult/SexualHealthReport04.pdf (accessed 7 July 2004)

Coffield, F., Moseley, D., Hall, E. and Ecclestone, K. (2004) 'Should we be using learning styles? What research has to say to practice' (online). Available from URL: www.lsrc.ac.uk/publications/index.asp (accessed 25 June 2007)

Condie, R., McPhee, A., Forde, C., Kane, J. and Head, G. (2005) *Review of Strategies to Address Gender Inequalities in Scottish Schools: Final Report*, Edinburgh: SEED

Connell, R.W. (1995) *Masculinities*, Cambridge: Polity Press

Connell, R.W. (2000) *The Men and the Boys*, Cambridge: Polity Press

Connell, R.W. (2002) *Gender*, Cambridge: Polity Press

Consultative Committee on the Curriculum (1983) *Primary Education in the Eighties – A COPE Position Paper*, Dundee: CCC

Consultative Committee on the Curriculum (1986) *Education in Scotland 10–14: A CCC Discussion Paper*, Dundee: CCC

Cook, M. (2005) '"A place of their own": creating a classroom "third space" to support a continuum of text construction between home and school', *Literacy*, Vol. 39, No. 2, pp. 85–90

Croxford, L. (1999) *Inequality in the First Year of Primary School*, CES Briefing No. 16, Edinburgh: Centre for Educational Sociology, University of Edinburgh

Croxford, L., Tinklin, T., Frame, B. and Ducklin, A. (2003) 'Gender and pupil performance: where do the problems lie?' *Scottish Educational Review*, Vol. 35, No. 2, pp. 135–47

Dart, B. C. and Clarke, J. A. (1988) 'Sexism in schools: a new look', *Educational Review*, Vol. 40, No. 1, pp. 41–9

Davies, J. and Brember, I. (1995) 'Attitudes to school and the curriculum in Year 2, Year 4 and Year 6: changes over 4 years', paper presented at the European Conference on Educational Research, Bath

Denholm, A. (2006) 'Girls still top of the class in exams', *The Herald*, Glasgow, 21 September

Department for Education and Science (1975) *A Language for Life*, Report of the Committee of Inquiry appointed by the Secretary of State for Education and Science (The Primary Memorandum), London: HMSO

Duffield, J. (2000) 'Gender in classrooms of more or less effective schools', in Salisbury, J. and Riddell, S. (eds) (2000) *Gender, Policy and Educational Change: Shifting Agendas in the UK and Europe*, London: Routledge, pp. 153–68

Epstein, D. (1998) 'Real boys don't work: "underachievement", masculinity and the harassment of "sissies" ', in Epstein, D., Ellwood, J., Hey, V. and Maw, J. (eds) (1998) *Failing Boys? Issues in Gender and Achievement*, Buckingham: Open University Press, pp. 96–108

Equal Opportunities Commission (2007) 'Gender Equality Duty: Guidance on the duty for pre-16 educational providers in Scotland' (online). Available from URL: www.eoc.org.uk/PDF/GED_SCottish_Pre-16_Education_Guidance.pdf (accessed 26 June 2007)

Felder, R. and Soloman, B. A. (1999) 'Index of learning styles' (online). Available from URL: www.ncsu.edu/felder-public/ILSpage.html (accessed 22 June 2007)

Felder, R. and Silverman, L. (1988) 'Learning and teaching styles in engineering education', *Engineering Education*, Vol. 78, No. 7, pp. 674–81

Forde, C., Kane, J., Condie, R., McPhee, A. and Head, G. (2005) *Strategies to Address Gender Inequalities in Scottish Schools: A Review of the Literature*, Edinburgh: SEED

Francis, B. (1999) 'Lads, lasses and "new" Labour: 14–16 year-old student responses to the "laddish behaviour and boys' underachievement" debate', *British Journal of Sociology of Education*, Vol. 20, No. 3, pp. 355–71

Francis, B. (2000) *Boys, Girls and Achievement: Addressing the Classroom Issues*, London: RoutledgeFalmer

Francis, B. (2005) 'Not/knowing their place: girls' classroom behaviour' in Lloyd, G. (ed.) (2005) *Problem Girls: Understanding and Supporting Troubled and Troublesome Girls and Young Women*, London: RoutledgeFalmer, pp. 9–22

Francis, B. and Skelton, C. (2001) *Investigating Gender: Contemporary Perspectives in Education*, Buckingham: Open University Press

Fraser, L. and Ross, K. (2004) 'Discovering reading together', *Literacy Today*, September, p. 8

Freire, P. (1970) *Pedagogy of the Oppressed*, New York: Continuum

Freire, P. (1994) *Pedagogy of Hope: Reliving Pedagogy of the Oppressed*, New York: Continuum

French, J. and French, P. (1984) 'Gender imbalances in the classroom: an interactional account', *Educational Research*, Vol. 26, No. 2, pp. 127–36

Frosh, S., Phoenix, A. and Pattman, R. (2003) 'The trouble with boys', *The Psychologist*, Vol. 16, No. 2, pp. 84–92

Fullan, M. (2005) *Leadership and Sustainability*, Thousand Oaks, CA: Corwin Press

Gilligan, C. (1982) *In a Different Voice: Psychological Theory and Women's Development*, London: Harvard University Press

Glasgow, University of (2006) University of Glasgow Archives (online). Available from URL: www.archives.gla.ac.uk/collects/catalog/dc/201-250/dc233.html (accessed 12 Oct. 2006)

Good, T., Cooper, H. and Blakely, S. (1980) 'Classroom interaction as function of teacher expectations, student sex and time of year', *Journal of Educational Psychology*, Vol. 72, pp. 378–85

Gorard, S., Rees, G., and Salisbury, J. (2001) 'Investigating the patterns of differential attainment of boys and girls at school', *British Educational Research Journal*, Vol. 27, No. 2, pp. 125–39

Gray, J. and McLellan, R. (2006) 'A matter of attitude? Developing a profile of boys' and girls' responses to primary schooling', *Gender and Education*, Vol. 18, No. 6, pp. 651–72

Hamilton, L. (2002) 'Constructing pupil identity: personhood and ability', *British Educational Research Journal*, Vol. 28, No. 4, pp. 591–602

Hamilton, L. (2006) 'Implicit theories of ability: teacher constructs and classroom consequences', *Scottish Educational Review*, Vol. 38, No. 2, pp. 200–211

Haywood, C. and Mac An Ghaill, M. (2006) 'Education and gender identity: seeking frameworks of understanding' in Arnot, M. and Mac An ghaill, M. (eds.) *The Routledge Falmer Reader in Gender and Education*. Oxford and New York: Routledge. 49–57.

Head, G. (2005) 'Better learning – better behaviour', *Scottish Educational Review*, Vol. 37, No. 2, pp. 94–103

Head, G., Kane, J. and Cogan, N. (2002) *An Evaluation of Behaviour Support in Secondary Schools in South Lanarkshire*, Glasgow: University of Glasgow

Head, G. and Jamieson, S. (2006) 'Taking a line for a walk: including school refusers', *Pastoral Care in Education*, Vol. 24, No. 3, pp. 32–40

Hogan, P. (2005) 'The politics of identity and the epiphanies of learning', in Carr, W. (ed.) (2005) *Philosophy of Education*, London: Routledge, pp. 83–96

Houston, B. (1994) 'Should public education be gender free?', in Stone, L. (ed.) (1994) *The Education Feminism Reader*, New York and London: Routledge, pp. 122–34

Houston, R. A. (1985) *Scottish Literacy and the Scottish Identity: Illiteracy and Society in Scotland and Northern England 1600–1800*, Cambridge: Cambridge University Press

Howe, C. (1997) *Gender and Classroom Interaction: A Research Review*, Edinburgh: Scottish Council for Research in Education

Humes, W. (2005) 'The discourse of community in educational policy', *Education in the North*, No. 12, pp. 6–13

Hunter, L. S. (1972) *The Scottish Educational System*, Oxford: Pergamon

Jackson, C. (2002) '"Laddishness" as a self-worth protection strategy', *Gender and*

Education, Vol. 14, No. 1, pp. 37–51

Jackson, D. (1998) 'Breaking out of the binary trap: boys' underachievement, schooling and gender relations', in Epstein, D., Ellwood, J., Hey, V. and Maw, J. (eds) (1998) *Failing Boys? Issues in Gender and Achievement*, Buckingham: Open University Press, pp. 77–95

Jones, S. and Myhill, D. (2004) '"Troublesome boys" and "compliant girls": gender identity and perceptions of achievement and underachievement', *British Journal of Sociology of Education*, Vol. 25, No. 2, pp. 547–61

Keddie, A. (2006) 'Pedagogies and critical reflection: key understandings for transformative gender justice', *Gender and Education*, Vol. 18, No. 1, pp. 99–114

Keefe, J. W. (1979) *Student Learning Styles: Diagnosing and Prescribing Programs*, Reston, VA: National Association of Secondary School Principals

Kehler, M. and Greig, C. (2005) 'Reading masculinities: exploring the socially literate practices of high school young men', *International Journal of Inclusive Education*, Vol. 9, No. 4, pp. 351–70

Kenway, J., Willis, S., Blackmore, J. and Rennie, L. (1998) *Answering Back: Girls, Boys and Feminism in Schools*, London: Routledge

Kenway, J. (2004) 'Gender reforms in schools: slip-sliding away', paper for Our A(gender): Demanding Equality, Australian Education Union Women's Conference, Melbourne, 2–3 October

Kerdeman, D. (2003) 'Pulled up short: challenging self-understanding as a focus of teaching and learning', *Journal of Philosophy of Education*, Vol. 32, No. 2, pp. 293–308

Kolb, D. (1984) *Experiential Learning: Experience as the Source of Learning and Development*, Englewood Cliffs, NJ: Prentice-Hall

Lingard, B. (2003) 'Where to in gender policy in education after recuperative masculinity politics?', *International Journal of Inclusive Education*, Vol. 7, No. 1, pp. 733–56

Lingard, B., Mills, M. and Hayes, D. (2000) 'Teachers, school reform and social justice: challenging research and practice', *Australian Educational Researcher*, Vol. 27, No. 3, pp. 93–109

Mac An Ghaill, M. (1988) *Young, Gifted and Black: Student–Teacher Relations in the Schooling of Black Youth.* Milton Keynes: Open University Press

Mac An Ghaill, M. (1994) *The Making of Men: Masculinities, Sexualities and Schooling*, Buckingham: Open University Press

Macrae, S. and Maguire, M. (2000) 'All change, no change: gendered regimes in the post-16 setting curricula', in Salisbury, J. and Riddell, S. (eds) (2000) *Gender, Policy and Educational Change: Shifting Agendas in the UK and Europe*, London: Routledge, pp. 169–85

Macaulay, C. (1790) 'Letters on education', in Todd, J. (ed.) (1996) *Female Education in the Age of Enlightenment Volume 1*, London: William Pickering

Maccoby, E. E., and Jacklin, C. N. (1975). *The Psychology of Sex Differences*, Stanford, CA: Stanford University Press

MacDonald, A., Saunders, L. and Benefield, P. (1999) *Boys' Achievement, Progress, Motivation and Participation: Issues Raised by the Recent Literature*, Slough: National Foundation for Educational Research

Maher, F. A. and Tetreault, M. K. T. (1994) *The Feminist Classroom*, New York: Basic Books

Martino, W. and Berrill, D. (2003) 'Boys, schooling and masculinities: interrogating the "right" way to educate boys', *Educational Review*, Vol. 55, No. 2, pp. 99–117

McLaughlin, C. (2005) 'Exploring the psycho-social landscape of "problem" girls: embodiment, relationship and agency', in Lloyd, G. (ed.) (2005) *'Problem Girls': Understanding and Supporting Troubled and Troublesome Girls and Young Women*, London: RoutledgeFalmer, pp. 51–62

McPhee, A. D. (1996) 'Policy, curriculum and the teaching of English language in the primary school', unpublished PhD thesis, University of Glasgow

Mills, M. (2001) *Challenging Violence in Schools*, Buckingham and Philadelphia: Open University Press

Mills, M., Martino, W. and Lingard, B. (2007) 'Getting boys' education "right": the Australian government's Parliamentary Inquiry Report as an exemplary instance of recuperative masculinity politics', *British Journal of Sociology of Education*, Vol. 28, No. 1, pp. 5–21

Morgan, V. and Dunn, S. (1988) 'Chameleons in the classroom: visible and invisible children in nursery and infant classrooms', *Educational Review*, Vol. 40, No. 1, pp. 3–12

Murphy, P. and Elwood, J. (1999) 'Failing Boys', in Epstein, D., Elwood, J. Hey, V. and Maw, J. (eds) (1999) *Failing Boys: Issues in Gender and Achievement*, Buckingham: Open University Press

Myhill, D. (2002) 'Bad boys and good girls? patterns of interaction and response in whole class teaching', *British Educational Research Journal*, Vol. 28, No. 3, pp. 339–52

National Priorities (2007) 'Priority 1 resources' (online). Available from URL www.nationalpriorities.org.uk/themes/themeList.php?theme=I (accessed 12 September 2007)

Newman, E. (2005) 'Lads and English', *English in Education*, Vol. 38, No. 1, pp. 32–42

Noble, C. and Bradford, W. (2000) *Getting it Right for Boys . . . and Girls*, London: Routledge

Oakley, A. (1972) *Gender and Society*, London: Temple Smith

Ornstein, A. C. and Levine, D. U. (1994). *Foundations of Education*, Boston: Houghton Mifflin

Osborn, M. (2004) 'New methodologies for comparative research: establishing 'constants' and 'contexts' in educational experience', *Oxford Review of Education*, Vol. 30, No. 2, pp. 265–85

Osler, A., Street, C., Lall, M. and Vincent, K. (2002) *Not a Problem? Girls and School Exclusion*, London: National Children's Bureau

Osler, A. and Vincent, K. (2003) *Girls and Exclusion: Rethinking the Agenda*, London: RoutledgeFalmer

Paechter, C. (1998) *Educating the Other: Gender, Power and Schooling*, London: Falmer Press

Paechter, C. (2006) 'Reconceptualizing the gendered body: learning and constructing masculinities and femininities in school', *Gender and Education*, Vol. 18, No. 2, pp. 121–35

Pahl, K. and Kelly, S. (2005) 'Family literacy as a third space between home and school: some case studies of practice ', *Literacy*, Vol. 39, No. 2, pp. 91–6

Paterson, L. (2003) *Scottish Education in the Twentieth Century*, Edinburgh: Edinburgh University Press

Plummer, G. (2000) *Failing Working Class Girls*, Stoke-on Trent: Trentham Books

Pollard, A. (1987) 'Goodies, Jokers and Gangs' in Pollard, A. (ed.) (1987) *Children and Their Primary Schools: A New Perspective*, Lewes: Falmer Press, pp. 165–87

Prashnig, B. (1998) *The Power of Diversity*, Auckland: David Bateman

Raphael Reed, L. (1999) 'Troubling boys and disturbing discourses on masculinity and schooling: a feminist exploration of current debates and interventions concerning boys in school', *Gender and Education*, Vol. 11, No. 1, pp. 93–110

Reading is Fundamental (2006) www.rif.org.uk (accessed 18 October 2006)

Read Together (2006) www.readtogether.co.uk (accessed 18 October 2006)

Reay, D. (1990) 'Girls' groups as a component of anti-sexist practice – one primary school's experience', *Gender and Education*, Vol. 2, No. 1, pp. 37–47

Reay, D. (2001) '"Spice Girls", "nice girls", "girlies" and "tomboys": gender discourses, girls' culture and femininities in the primary classroom', *Gender and Education*, Vol. 13, No. 2, pp. 153–66

Reay, D. (2002) 'Shaun's story: troubling discourses of white, working-class' masculinities', *Gender and Education*, Vol. 14, No. 3, pp. 221–34

Reay, D. (2006) '"I'm not seen as one of the clever children": consulting primary school pupils about the social conditions of learning', *Educational Review*, Vol. 58, No. 2, pp. 171–81

Reay, D. and Wiliam, D. (1999) '"I'll be a nothing": structure, agency and the construction of identity through assessment [1]', *British Educational Research Journal*, Vol. 25, No. 3, pp. 343–54

Renold, E. (2004) 'Other' boys: negotiating non-hegemonic masculinities in the primary school', *Gender and Education*, Vol. 16, No. 2, pp. 247–66

Riddell, S. (2000) 'Equal opportunities and educational reform in Scotland: the limits of liberalism', in Salisbury, J. and Riddell, S. (eds) (2000) *Gender, Policy and Educational Change: Shifting Agendas in the UK and Europe*, London: Routledge

Riddell, S., Tett, L., Burns, C., Ducklin, A., Ferrie, J., Stafford, A and Winterton, M. (2005) *Gender Balance of the Teaching Workforce in Publicly Funded Schools*, Edinburgh: University of Edinburgh

Riding, R. and Rayner, S. (1998) *Cognitive Styles and Learning Strategies: Understanding Style Differences in Learning and Behaviour*, London: David Fulton

Rowe, K., Nix, P. J. and Tepper, G. (1996) 'Single-sex and mixed-sex classes: the joint effects of class type on student performance in attitudes towards mathematics', paper presented at the Annual Conference of the Australian Association for Research in Education, Melbourne

Rowe, K. (1998) 'Single-sex and mixed-sex classes: the effects of class type on student achievement', *Australian Journal of Education*, Vol. 32, No. 2, pp. 180–202

Ruddick, S. (1990) *Maternal Thinking: Towards a Politics of Peace*, London: The Women's Press

Rudduck, J. and Urquhart, I. (2003) 'Some neglected issues of transfer: identity, status and gender from the pupils' perspective', in Skelton, C. and Francis, B. (eds) (2003), *Boys and Girls in the Primary Classroom*, Maidenhead: Open University Press, pp. 167–85

Scottish Education Department (1950) *The Primary School in Scotland*, Edinburgh: HMSO

Scottish Education Department (1965) *Primary Education in Scotland*, Edinburgh: HMSO

Scottish Executive (2000) *The Education (National Priorities) (Scotland) Order 2000*, Edinburgh: The Stationery Office

Scottish Executive (2007a) *Exclusions from School 2005/6*, Edinburgh: Scottish Executive National Statistics Publication

Scottish Executive (2007b) *Teachers in Scotland, 2006 Statistical Publication: Education Series (Edn/G5/2007/2)*, Edinburgh: Scottish Executive

Scottish Executive Education Department (2001) *Gender and Pupil Performance*, *Interchange 70*, Edinburgh: Scottish Executive

Scottish Executive Education Department (2004) 'A Curriculum for Excellence: Curriculum Review Group' (online). Available from URL: www.scotland.gov.uk/Resource/Doc/26800/0023690.pdf (accessed 15 March 2007)

Scottish Executive Education Department (2005) *Scottish Survey of Achievement: English Language and Core Skills*, Edinburgh: SEED

Scottish Office (1998) 'National Year of Reading in Scotland' (online). Available from URL www.scotland.gov.uk/library/documents5/rd01.htm?2;news/releas98_1/pr1319.htm (accessed 12 Ocober 2006)

Scottish Office Education Department (1991) *Curriculum and Assessment in Scotland; National Guidelines 5–14 in English Language*, Edinburgh: HMSO

Skelton, C. (1996) 'Learning to be tough: the fostering of maleness in one primary school', *Gender and Education*, Vol. 8, No. 2, pp. 185–97

Skelton, C. (1997) 'Primary boys and hegemonic masculinities', *British Journal of Sociology of Education*, Vol. 18, No. 3, pp. 349–69

Skelton, C. (2001) *Schooling the Boys: Masculinities and Primary Education*, Buckingham: Open University Press

Skelton, C. (2002) 'The "feminisation" of schooling or "re-masculinising" primary education?', *International Studies in Sociology of Education*, Vol. 12, No. 1, pp. 77–96

Skelton, C. (2003) 'Male primary teachers and perceptions of masculinity', *Educational Review*, Vol. 50, No. 2, pp. 195–209

Smith I. and De Felice H. (2001) *Boys are Different . . . or are they?* Glasgow: Learning Unlimited

Smith, V. and Ellis, S. (2005) *A Curriculum for Excellence: Review of Research Literature: Language and Literacy*, Glasgow: University of Strathclyde

Solsken, J. W. (1993) *Literacy, Gender and Work in Families and School*, Norwood, NJ: Ablex Publishing

Sommers, C. H. (2000) *The War against Boys: How Misguided Feminism is Harming our Young Men*, New York: Simon and Schuster

Spender, D. (1982) *Invisible Women: The Schooling Scandal*, London: Writers and Readers

Squire, C. (1989) *Significant Differences: Feminism in Psychology*, London: Routledge and Kegan Paul

Stanworth, M. (1983) *Gender and Schooling: A Study of Sexual Divisions in the Classroom*, London: Hutchinson

Strand, S. (1997) 'Pupil progress during Key Stage 1: a value added analysis of school effects', *British Educational Research Journal*, Vol. 23, No. 4, pp. 471–88

Strange, V., Oakley, A. and Forrest, S. (2003) 'Mixed-sex or single-sex sex education', *Gender and Education*, Vol. 15, No. 2, pp. 201–14

Sukhnandan L., Lees. B., and Kelleher, S. (2000) *An Investigation into Gender Differences in Achievement: Phase 2: School and Classroom Strategies*, Slough: National Foundation for Educational Research

Swann, J. and Graddol, D. (1988) 'Gender inequalities in classroom talk', *English in Education*, Vol. 22, No.1, pp. 48–65.

Tett, L. and Riddell, S. (eds) (2006) *Gender and Teaching: Where Have All the Men Gone?* Edinburgh: Dunedin Academic Press

Tinklin, T., Croxford, L., Ducklin, A. and Frame, B. (2001) *Gender and Pupil Performance in Scotland's Schools*, Edinburgh: Scottish Executive Education Department

Tinklin, T. (2003) 'Gender differences and high Attainment', *British Educational Research Journal*, Vol. 29, No. 3, pp. 307–24

Torsi, S. (2005) 'Champion dads', *Literacy Today*, March, p. 13

Warin, J. (2006) 'Heavy-metal Humpty Dumpty: dissonant masculinities within the context of the nursery', *Gender and Education*, Vol. 18, No. 5, pp. 523–37

Warrington, M. and Younger, M. (2001) ' "We decided to give it a twirl": Single sex teaching in English comprehensive schools', *Gender and Education*, Vol. 15, No. 4, pp. 339–50

Warrington, M. and Younger, M. (2003) 'Single-sex classes and equal opportunities for girls and for boys: perspective through time from a mixed comprehensive school in England', *Oxford Review of Education*, Vol. 27, No. 3, pp. 339–56

Whyte, J. (1984) 'Observing sex stereotypes and interactions in the school lab and workshop', *Educational Review*, Vol. 36, No. 1, pp. 75–86

Whyte, J. (1986) *Girls into Science and Technology*, London: Routledge and Kegan Paul

Willis, P. (1978) *Learning to Labour: How Working-Class Kids Get Working-Class Jobs*, Aldershot: Ashgate

Wilkinson, J. E., Napuk, A., Watt, J., Normand, B. and Johnson, S. (1999) *The Development of Baseline Assessment in Scotland: Pilot Procedures: Final Report*, Edinburgh: Scottish Executive Education Department

Woodhead, C. (1996) 'Boys who learn to be losers', *The Times*, 6 March

Younger, M. and Warrington, M (2004) *Raising Boys' Achievement: A Study Funded by the Department for Education and Skills*, DfES Research Report RR63, Cambridge: University of Cambridge

INDEX